Sabine Baring-Gould

Sabine Baring-Gould

SQUARSON, WRITER AND FOLKLORIST, 1834-1924

by

BICKFORD H. C. DICKINSON

DAVID & CHARLES : NEWTON ABBOT

7153 4803 5

COPYRIGHT NOTICE

© BICKFORD H. C. DICKINSON 1970

All rights reserved. No part of this publication may be reproduced, stored in a retrieval system, or transmitted, in any form or by any means, electronic, mechanical, photocopying, recording or otherwise, without the prior permission of David & Charles (Publishers) Limited

*Set in 11 point Baskerville 2 point leaded and
Printed in Great Britain by
Bristol Typesetting Company Limited
Barton Manor St Philips Bristol
for David & Charles (Publishers) Limited
South Devon House Newton Abbot Devon*

Contents

	Foreword	11
1	The Genteel Vagabonds	13
2	Learning and Teaching	28
3	The Curate of Horbury Brig	42
4	Dalton i't Muck	51
5	The Rector of East Mersea	61
6	Home at Last	75
7	The Rector of Lew Trenchard	91
8	The Squarson	104
9	A Lantern for my Christ	117
10	The Old Singing Men	123
11	The Man of Letters	141
12	The Eagle's Nest	161
13	'Now the Day is Over'	170
	Bibliography	176
	Abridged Genealogical Tree	186
	Index	187

List of Illustrations

	Page
Sabine Baring-Gould, at the age of 68	17
Sabine Baring-Gould, aged 86	17
Sabine Baring-Gould setting out on his morning round of visits	18
Sabine with his half-brother Arthur	18
Sabine, aged 88	35
Sabine in old age	35
Grace Baring-Gould, wife of Sabine	36
Mary Dickinson, eldest child of Sabine and Grace	36
Lew Trenchard Church	53
Lew House as it is today	54
The Lew Trenchard Menhir	54
The Wye Cottages	71
Dunsland, the home of Sabine's son-in-law, A. W. H. Dickinson	71
'The vagaries of clerical dress'	72

In Text

Richard Hard	132
John Helmore	133
The Baring-Gould's family tree	186

*It is the generous Spirit, who, when brought
Among the tasks of real life, hath wrought
Upon the plan that pleased his childish thought;
Whose high endeavours are an inward light
That makes the path before him always bright;
Who, with a natural instinct to discern
What knowledge can perform, is diligent to learn;
Abides by this resolve, and stops not there,
But makes his moral being his prime care.
. . .
And, while the mortal mist is gathering, draws
His breath in confidence of Heaven's applause
This is the Happy Warrior; this is he
Whom every man in arms should wish to be.*
                              William Wordsworth

FOREWORD

There are men who become almost legendary figures even during their own lifetime. This seems to have little to do with fame or greatness, for there have been famous men of whom no legends are told, and others with no possible claim to being considered great about whom stories accumulate. The chief qualification seems to be that of being so unusual that the most exaggerated stories become believable.

Sabine Baring-Gould, parson, squire, hymn-writer, novelist and antiquarian, was certainly unusual; about him there have grown up a number of legends—so many in fact that it is often hard to separate truth from fiction. Many articles have been written about him and his work and he has been quoted and referred to in several books, but perhaps the best and most accurate short account of him is to be found in *The English Parson* by William Addison, published in 1947. A full-length and detailed biography by William Purcell was published under the title *Onward, Christian Soldier* in 1957, and the revival of interest in folk songs keeps his name alive today. But in none of the above books, admirable as some of them are, is the Sabine Baring-Gould whom they depict quite like the man still personally remembered by a dwindling number of elderly people, including myself.

My excuse for telling again the story of his life is that I have many sources of information denied to previous writers. In the first place, I have my own vivid memories of him, for I stayed at Lew House on many occasions as a boy and young man and I was twenty-four years old when he died. From my mother, his

Foreword

eldest child, I heard countless anecdotes of the family life of the Baring-Goulds, going back to the far-off days when Sabine was rector of East Mersea. My elder brother, Arscott Dickinson, seven years my senior, has supplied me with personal memories of his own. I have at my disposal the copious notes made by Sabine's seventh daughter, the late Mrs Joan Priestley, and also a very interesting account of him and his wife Grace, sent me by Mrs Irene Widdicombe, the daughter of Sabine's half-brother Arthur. Most valuable of all, I possess a very large collection of Sabine's letters to my mother, discovered in her desk after her death. The earliest of these dates from 1889, the year of her marriage, and the last was written only a few weeks before his death.

Lastly, I was myself rector of Lew Trenchard parish for six years and he was still remembered there by a number of the older generation. I would like to express my particular gratitude to the memory of the late Mrs Northey and the late Mr Arthur Westington, from whom I heard many stories of Sabine's acts of spontaneous kindness, his impulsiveness and his undoubted peculiarities.

My sincere thanks are due to the many kind people who, in answer to correspondence in the press, have supplied me with a mass of interesting old newspaper cuttings, photographs, letters and personal memories.

B. H. C. DICKINSON

I

The Genteel Vagabonds

Between the years 1834, in which Sabine Baring-Gould was born, and 1924, in which he died, there stretches a vast gulf. The changes that took place during those ninety years were so profound and their results so far-reaching that it is hard to realise that one man's life could have spanned them all.

Sabine was born into a slow-moving world in which the horse and the sailing ship constituted the only regular means of travel on land and sea, for steam transport was still in its infancy. Yet before his death the Atlantic had been crossed in an aeroplane and the motor car had already begun to imperil the supremacy not only of the carriage horse but of the railways.

It was during his lifetime that the care of children, the sick and the destitute, which in his youth had been left almost entirely to individual charity, grew to be recognised as the moral responsibility of the whole community. He was born a member of the old, privileged, landowning class to whom the demands of the Chartists for manhood suffrage and equal political rights seemed dangerously subversive. Yet before his death every adult had received the right to vote. It was during his lifetime, too, that the struggle for free education for all was fought and won, while at the same time, as new scientific discoveries changed men's outlook on the universe, most of the long-accepted religious dogmas were first openly questioned. It is only against this widely changing background that we can begin to gauge the value, or in any way assess the qualities of Sabine Baring-Gould and his contemporaries.

The Goulds were typical of those small landowning families who exercised so much influence on English history during the seventeenth and eighteenth centuries and from whose ranks were drawn almost exclusively the members of the House of Commons, the officers of the armed forces of the Crown, the clergy of the established Church, and the lawyers, magistrates and judges who administered the law.

As was common at that time the Goulds laid claim to 'Norman blood' and traced their pedigree from a certain thirteenth-century crusader called John Gold; the first authentic historical evidence we have of them, however, is when in the early sixteenth century they acquired property in Staverton in Devon. During the seventeenth century they became successfully involved in trading ventures which much increased their prosperity. One of the family, James Gould, a Leghorn merchant, was made mayor of Exeter in 1648. During his period of office he championed the Royalist cause and was responsible for saving Exeter Cathedral from being plundered by Cromwell's forces. His relative, Colonel William Gould, on the other hand, defended Plymouth for Parliament against Royalist attacks on the town. Meanwhile another relative, Henry Gould, had purchased the manor of Lew Trenchard from its former owner, Sir Thomas Monk, in 1626. The fortunes of this branch of the family fluctuated considerably. In 1767 Captain Edward Gould inherited the estate and before his death in 1788 he had succeeded in dissipating most of the family wealth by gambling. Lew House, however, was not his to dispose of and it was saved, together with the remnant of the estate, by the energy of his mother, a redoubtable old lady usually referred to as 'Old Madam Gould'; she became a local legend and her ghost is still said to haunt the house and grounds, though she seems to have become less active since the installation of electric light.

The family fortunes again improved when her daughter Margaret married Charles Baring, a member of the wealthy banking house of that name. It was their son William who first doubled the surname and called himself Baring-Gould. William's method of providing for his sons followed the normal pattern of his class and time. For Edward, his eldest son, he purchased a commission in the armed forces of the East India Company. Alexander, his second son, was ordained and eventually became vicar of Wolverhampton, while Charles, the youngest, was also ordained and for him the family living of Lew Trenchard was reserved. He was presented to it immediately upon his ordination in 1832 and in it he drowsed peacefully for forty-nine years. Edward, however, met with an accident which necessitated his being invalided out of the army and returning to civilian life while still a young man. He arrived back in England in 1830 with a permanent limp and an incurable wanderlust.

It was the custom at that time to give a nickname to anyone of striking appearance. Captain Edward Baring-Gould, tall, slender and fair haired, was labelled 'the Silver Poplar'. Soon after his enforced return to England he married his first wife, a Miss Charlotte Bond, and tried to settle down in the parish of Bratton Clovelly, near to his family home at Lew Trenchard. He soon became hopelessly bored by rural life and the company of his few neighbours, whose only interests lay in field sports for which he cared nothing. In desperation he finally bought a carriage, engaged a coachman and in 1837 commenced a career of genteel vagabondage which was to last almost continuously until 1851.

The Genteel Vagabonds

When in the spring of 1837 Edward Baring-Gould and his wife set off in their carriage, driven by Pengelly their coachman, it contained themselves and their first two children, of whom Sabine was the elder, a nurse and all their luggage, including the family silver. Thus equipped they meandered through Europe, returning to England only very occasionally and then only for short periods. In consequence the child Sabine had an extraordinary upbringing. Between the ages of three and sixteen he spent less than three years in his native land.

If the England of those days seems to us very far away, Europe was infinitely more so. Beneath the surface the bitter discontent that led to 'the Year of Revolutions' in 1848, was already seething, but outwardly at least the old order, re-established by the Congress of Vienna in 1815, seemed firmly in the saddle. The shade of Prince Metternich, the principal creator of the Holy Alliance and the apostle of reaction, still brooded over the Europe through which the Baring-Gould carriage made its leisurely progress.

Every year Edward Baring-Gould and his family would spend the winter in some favoured spot within easy reach of the English mail. This was vitally important as Edward was a great reader and expected to receive regularly each monthly instalment of Mr Charles Dickens' latest novel.* Then each spring they would move on again. Sometimes they journeyed down ancient highways, making their sedate progress down roads that had felt the tread of Roman Legions. At other times the iron-bound wheels of their carriage rolled smoothly along the military roads of Napoleon's creation. Yet again they would jolt and sway along deeply rutted tracks, when Mrs Baring-Gould would suffer uncomplaining agonies of discomfort. Then at last they would pause a while—a month, three months, for time was no object—and then on again.

From whom Sabine received his primary education it is hard

* *Early Reminiscences.*

Page 17: *Sabine Baring-Gould, at the age of 68. (Pencil drawing by Constance Mortimore). Mary Dickinson, his daughter, thought this the best likeness.*
(National Portrait Gallery)

Sabine Baring Gould, aged 86. Portrait by Melton Fisher, RA. Of this picture Sabine wrote, 'Yesterday I had the 8th and last of my sittings for my portrait, each 2½ hours long. Mr. Fisher has carried off the picture to Town where it will be photographed and you will receive a copy. The painting has to be exhibited in the Royal Academy so we shall not have it till the end of July. As a painting it is fine. Whether a likeness or not I am unable to judge. It is a picture of an old decrepit boat.'

Page 18: (above) *Sabine Baring-Gould setting out on his morning round of visits, driven by Charles Dustan;* (below) *Sabine with his half-brother Arthur, during a tramp on Dartmoor, probably about 1905.*

The Genteel Vagabonds

to say. Whether it was from his gentle, pious mother or from his autocratic, opinionated father we shall never know, but all the regular schooling he ever received was two years between 1844 and 1846 as a boarder at King's College School, London, and one year as a day-boy at Warwick Grammar School. Even this short spell of regular tuition was much curtailed, for he spent most of one winter in London in bed with congestion of the lungs, and the return of the trouble while he was attending Warwick Grammar School gave his father the excuse to be on the move again and take his whole family to the South of France.

In the course of years their leisurely tours took them through France, Belgium, Germany, Italy and Austria; past ancient cities and through little out-of-the-way villages, where the inhabitants had never before seen an Englishman and where life was still almost feudal.

So it came to pass that during the most formative years of his life, Sabine never knew a place that he could call home, never had the mental discipline of regular schooling and never learned to play one outdoor game. But he had the chance of cultivating his natural love of beauty, and by the age of fifteen he could speak five languages fluently.

At a time when grave and bewhiskered gentlemen, led by no less a person than the Prince Consort, were planning the Great Exhibition and dreaming of a scientific and political Utopia in the not too distant future, young Sabine was acquiring a tremendous veneration for the past. While still a boy he grew to reverence all things that seemed to him beautiful and to despise anything that did not. So to him beauty became synonymous with goodness and ugliness with evil. An ancient cathedral, a wayside shrine, a village church set amid forests; these were beautiful and right. A Lutheran chapel, like a factory, was in his eyes ugly and in consequence he never learned to see any real virtue in either.

There was, too, something else that he was unconsciously

The Genteel Vagabonds

absorbing. To English eyes the comparatively modest fortunes of the smaller landed gentry were becoming completely overshadowed by the newly-made wealth of the industrialists, but by continental standards English tourists like the Baring-Goulds were well-to-do, and this impression was greatly helped by the favourable rate of exchange.

The name of Englishman stood high in Europe at that time. It still carried with it some of the prestige engendered by British victories during the Napoleonic Wars. The type of Englishman who travelled abroad was often laughed at for his foibles, but was usually respected for his integrity. As a result of this attitude the greater part of Sabine's youth was spent in an atmosphere in which respectful service was accepted as a natural state of affairs. Just how far this influenced his outlook towards those with whom he came in contact in later life is not easy to assess, but from a close study of his books, especially his novels, it does seem to have influenced it to some extent.

It would probably have done so more deeply but for his mother's training. With her he regularly visited the sick and destitute in the terrible slums of the European towns through which they passed, and the sight of their neglect and misery did much to form his later advanced political views. Mrs Baring-Gould had been brought up in the old 'Lady Bountiful' tradition and visited the unfortunate regularly, with a basket of delicacies on her arm, just as naturally in a foreign land as she would have done at home. Under her guidance, Sabine acquired a deep sense of personal responsibility for the lot of the very poor, but it is doubtful if he ever quite learned to understand what was passing in their minds. His attitude when he wrote about them was always inclined to be a little aloof, and in this he resembled the majority of the Anglican clergy of his day, who were drawn almost exclusively from the ranks of the upper-middle class. These had from childhood been segregated by being sent away from home to one of the great public schools. From

The Genteel Vagabonds

there they went on to Oxford or Cambridge to read for a Classical degree. As André Maurois, that shrewd and kindly observer of English life, has written in his *History of England*:

> To take Holy Orders the Anglican cleric did not need to pass through a specifically theological college. An ordinary Oxford or Cambridge degree sufficed. Their culture, so far as they had one, was as much Classical as Christian. They were gentlemen with the tastes and failings, and the virtues too, of their class.

Such a system was bound to isolate even the best-intentioned parson from the majority of his parishioners, for during the formative years of his life his only possible contact with them was during the long school and university vacations and then it was probably confined to sharing in their field sports in winter and playing cricket for the village in summer. How strongly Sabine disapproved of such an upbringing will become obvious from the education that his own sons received, but in his own youth he was denied even the tenuous holiday contacts open to others, owing to his father's restless nature.

It was not until 1851, when Sabine was already seventeen, that Edward Baring-Gould finally returned to England. For a while he settled in Tavistock, a small market town some nine miles south of the little rural parish of Lew Trenchard, the manor house of which was the family home of the Baring-Goulds, and to which Sabine was to return thirty years later to be both squire and rector for the last forty-three years of his life.

The year 1851 was indeed a memorable and, as one looks back on it, in some ways a tragic one, for it saw the opening of the Great Exhibition, which marked the peak of Victorian optimism and faith in the newly revealed wonders of science. Here, men felt, was the symbol of that new world of lasting peace and prosperity that would surely be the outcome of progress, free trade and mutual understanding.

The Genteel Vagabonds

Sabine Baring-Gould was then at an age when uncritical enthusiasm for a cause is readily formed. But no dream of a peaceful, scientific Utopia seems to have entered his head; nor was he bedevilled by the grandiose visions engendered in so many minds by the sight of a rapidly expanding empire. In consequence, despite the fact that all the high hopes of a lasting world peace were soon to be shattered by the sailing of the troop-ships to the Crimea; although he would live to see the American Civil War, the Indian Mutiny, the Franco-Prussian War, the Boer War, the Russian-Japanese War, the Balkan War and finally the first World War, he was never to suffer the bitter disillusionment that was the lot of so many of his generation. He had not the type of mind that is readily interested in world movements. In his eyes history was not a matter of social or political trends, or even the story of the rise and decline of nations and empires. Rather it was the chronicle of individual persons and their achievements that fascinated him, whether they were saints or sinners, heroes or villains, writers, craftsmen or merely oddities. People interested him intensely, but not *the* people. It was the characters of the Caesars that seemed to him important and not the empire over which they ruled. Napoleon was a far more worthy subject for study than his campaigns.

Brought up largely in the company of adults, he matured early, and the strong tastes and prejudices which were to play so large a part in his life were forming while he was still a boy. At the age of barely fifteen, during a short stay in England brought about by the unsafe state of Europe during the Year of Revolutions, Sabine had visited Lew Trenchard, of which parish his Uncle Charles was then rector. Used as he was to the beauty of Roman Catholic churches on the Continent, the little parish church appalled him, for it had been the victim of a remarkable act of vandalism, perpetrated sixteen years previously. In 1832, in order to make it spruce and tidy for his youngest son, shortly to be instituted as rector, Sabine's grand-

The Genteel Vagabonds

father had swept away all the ancient oak pews and also the decaying but magnificent rood-screen, which had been the glory of the church. In their place he had installed deal 'horse-box' pews and a new deal pulpit, all of which were painted a bright mustard yellow. To heighten the effect the altar was adorned with a bright blue altar-cloth and the pulpit provided with blue hangings fringed with yellow. These colours had of course no liturgical significance, but were intended to remind all who came to worship what were the correct tinctures of the Baring-Gould coat-of-arms. Boy though he was, Sabine was shocked and disgusted.

Although nearly seventeen years had passed, he managed to find, forgotten in the belfry of the church and in the lumber-room and outbuildings of Lew House, a number of fragments of the old woodwork. In old age he would sometimes speak of how he had carefully hidden these away in order to preserve them, for even at the age of fifteen there was forming in his mind a plan that was to become one of the main objects of his life: the complete restoration of Lew Trenchard church.

During the following winter, when he had once more returned to France with his parents, he spent many weeks in the public library at Pau, translating Michaud's *History of the Crusades*. This was certainly a remarkable occupation to be undertaken on his own initiative by an active boy of fifteen, especially as his taste for the subject seems to have developed spontaneously without any encouragement. The past was always to have a profound interest for him, but at no period of his life was it an exclusive one, for he had the type of mind that ranges over a wide variety of subjects and never specialises on any one. Among the many hobbies of this solitary and unusual boy, who was later to be rather unkindly dubbed 'the man with the magpie mind', was field botany. This led him one day, while strolling down a country lane near Pau, to grub up a few wild-flower roots for further study. Beneath the flower roots he came upon

The Genteel Vagabonds

fragments of mosaic, which proved upon excavation to be part of a splendidly preserved floor of a Roman villa, some two hundred feet in length. With a quiet, natural authority that would brook no denial, he undertook responsibility for the whole 'dig', directing the French workmen himself and making careful notes and water-colour drawings of all he found. The English community in Pau were pleased and excited; a committee was formed and money raised for the preservation of what had been laid bare. Nineteen years later Sabine described the mosaic pavement in detail under the title 'Legends of the Cross', an illustrated article in his book *Curious Myths of the Middle Ages*.

His *Early Reminiscences* was not published until seventy-three years later, but even after that lapse of time he was still bitter at the fact that this, his first antiquarian discovery, was eventually not properly preserved, but, owing to the petty jealousies of the local French authorities, was allowed to disintegrate completely.

Now at the age of seventeen he was back in England and living at Tavistock. Dartmoor was almost at his door, and as was only natural after his success at Pau, its then almost completely unrecognised antiquities at once attracted him irresistibly, as did the austere beauty of what was then England's last almost unexplored wilderness. With his long legs astride a shaggy Dartmoor pony he began a quest which was to last off and on for the rest of his life, for Dartmoor was always to fascinate him. He was to spend many hundreds of hours roaming its wide, heather-clad expanse and he was to write many thousands of words about all that he found there. If at times he jumped to conclusions upon insufficient data, and if some of the work that he did had little of the scientific exactitude displayed by the modern archaeologist, this reflects the fact that he never had any training in either history or archaeology as an exact science. But to the study of the Moor he brought, as he did to everything else in life, a tremendous enthusiasm and an enormous energy.

The Genteel Vagabonds

To his generation all megalithic standing stones, dolmens and stone circles, were the work of the Druids and all earthworks were Roman camps. Their use and origin had given rise to much romantic speculation, but no serious investigation of them had been attempted. A few barrows had been opened by treasure-seekers and, where they were accessible, a considerable number of megalithic stones had been broken up for road metal; otherwise the prehistoric monuments were merely matters for local superstition and for the most part had remained untouched. The serious study of those on Dartmoor was not undertaken by Sabine until nearly forty years later, when he and his great friend Robert Burnard spent several years in examining them closely, but his interest in them was undoubtedly first aroused during his stay in Tavistock in 1851.

Prior to that time only two men seem to have shown any real interest in this direction, the Rev Edward Atkyns Bray, vicar of Tavistock, and Samuel Rowe. Bray examined such remains as he could visit conveniently on foot from a house that he built at Bairdown, above Two Bridges, and the results of his investigations were published in 1836 under the title *Borders of the Tamar and Tavy*, a book written by his wife and consisting of a series of letters to Robert Southey. Samuel Rowe made a fuller and more systematic exploration, the results of which were published in 1848 in his book *Perambulations of Dartmoor*. Sabine had no very high opinion of the powers of observation or deduction displayed by either Bray or Rowe. In his *Early Reminiscences* he wrote somewhat sarcastically of their work and claimed for Robert Burnard and himself the sole credit for proving that the ancient stone monuments were neither Celtic or Druidic, but belonged to the Bronze Age.

Sometimes he would be away from home for several days at a time, spending the nights in remote moorland taverns, where he would sit quietly in a corner and listen to the songs sung by the moormen; the quaint old traditional folk melodies, which

The Genteel Vagabonds

in years to come were to add one more to the long list of interests that filled his life.

With his natural gift for languages and his reverence for the past, Sabine would, with proper training, undoubtedly have developed into a good classical scholar, but he was never given the chance. It is ironic that at a period when the public schools provided little but an undiluted classical fare, and when a sound knowledge of Greek and Latin was still widely regarded as the best possible training for life, he was only encouraged by his father to study mathematics; Edward Baring-Gould held strong views on a number of subjects, one of which was education. He was quite convinced that the human mind in youth was a sponge, capable of absorbing whatever was poured into it. Having succumbed to the popular worship of the machine as the cure for all human ills, he was equally convinced that mathematics provided the key to all useful knowledge. In consequence Sabine, before entering Cambridge University in 1853, was sent for a period of private coaching to the Rev Harvey Goodwin, incumbent of St Edward's church, Cambridge, because Goodwin had been Second Wrangler and had the reputation for being a first-class mathematical coach. With Sabine, however, he was a complete failure, for his pupil's mind, though in some ways encyclopaedic, became an absolute blank when confronted with the simplest problem in mathematics. This weakness Sabine was always the first to admit: 'Goodwin was a good, kind man,' he wrote, 'and took infinite pains with me. . . . He got me as far as Euler's proof for the Binomial Theorem. But what that theorem was, and of what good its solution could be to humanity, I have not the slightest idea. . . . At the present day, in addition, I have to use my fingers for counting, and in compound addition, I have to take my bills into the kitchen, and get one of the servant maids to do the calculation for me.'

For Goodwin as a clergyman Sabine had little respect, for he was a typical Low Churchman of his day and of such Sabine

The Genteel Vagabonds

was always critical, to say the least. Yet it was Goodwin who was asked to prepare Sabine for confirmation. Somehow his faith survived the ordeal, though he received no definite instruction whatever and he was confirmed at a service that was singularly lacking both in dignity and reverence.

Eventually his disappointed father gave up all idea of making a mathematician out of him, and he was grudgingly permitted to enter Clare Hall, Cambridge, as a Classical student.

2

Learning and Teaching

At Cambridge Sabine went his own way. That at first he was regarded as crazy by his fellow undergraduates probably worried him little enough, as all his life he was singularly immune to the influence of public opinion. He must have seemed a strange and incomprehensible figure to the games-playing young public school men among whom he was thrown. Tall, forceful, with the dominating personality sometimes associated with great mental and physical energy, he was strikingly good-looking, as his portraits show. This in itself might tend to be a barrier with other young men. Far more so would have been the fact that he was openly devout, though he always had an outspoken contempt for the dreary preaching that at that time characterised most Anglican services. In his *Early Reminiscences* he quotes a fellow spirit as saying: 'I have heard a thousand and fifty-three sermons, and, thank God, I am still a Christian.'

Sabine was always curiously reticent about the development of his religious beliefs during his youth. Most of the Baring-Goulds at that time seem to have been Evangelical Low Churchmen. His father and his uncle Alexander certainly were, but his mother practised Christianity after the old High Church tradi-

Learning and Teaching

tion and regulated her life by a fixed timetable of prayer, alms-giving and good works. Sabine was undoubtedly influenced by her teaching and example, by his natural love of dignified and traditional ceremonial and by his dislike of the Lutheran form of worship that he had encountered on his travels. By the time that he went to Cambridge he was ready to be caught up in the second wave of the Tractarian Movement that was then sweeping the universities, despite the hostility of the press and of the Government, which, to quote the *Oxford Dictionary of the Christian Church* 'chose the majority of bishops from the ranks of its opponents'. Here, too, is a clue to Sabine's later attacks and sarcastic references to most of his ecclesiastical superiors.

He had, too, begun to accumulate a vast if ill-digested store of unusual information, and his wanderings had given him the mastery of five languages, then as now an unusual accomplishment in an Englishman. In the sport and outdoor games that form so large a part of university life he took not the slightest interest.

Such an unusual person might well have come in for a certain amount of 'ragging', but throughout his life Sabine had something strangely formidable about him that would have discouraged horseplay. Together with a few others he soon formed what would at that time have been called a 'Holy Club', and after a while he collected round him a number of followers and admirers. One of these, Samuel Brierly, wrote in 1855 a letter to his sister describing their activities.

23 February 1855.
I have just returned from King's College Chapel, where Chawner, myself, Martin of Corpus and Gould of Clare Hall have entered into a bond to go every Wednesday and Friday during this holy season, instead of attending dinner in Hall. I cannot tell you how it is, but I feel a great satisfaction in practising this 'very little amount of self-denial' as Martin calls it. I can assure you that these two new friends of mine are the most perfect patterns of

Learning and Teaching

Christians and Catholics I ever saw.... Gould is a tall, thin, pale man, in fact like Mr Sharpe, though without his sternness. I dare say you will smile at what I am going to say, but I care not, for you would say the same if you saw him. He has the sweetest face I ever saw in my life, always serene and undisturbed, with an almost supernatural brightness about it. In fact, I never saw a face anything like it in my life. When we first came up to Cambridge, because he kept his chapels with unvarying punctuality, stayed away from Hall two or three times a week to attend service at King's, was known to spend much of his time in devotion, and much of his money in almsgiving, and conducting himself altogether according to his faith, he was called mad. But two years have passed, and his former revilers (none he has now), find him pursuing the course which he started, and very many of them follow his example. He is well known to all the orthodox clergy of Cambridge and is universally beloved by them, and by the undergraduates who really know him.

Even allowing for a great deal of youthful hero-worship, this is a remarkable letter, it has been quoted here because it is the only contemporary account that we have of Sabine at this period of his life. It was first seen by Sabine when he was a very old man and it provided the sad comment: 'This is all very exaggerated and extravagant. If in any way true, and I doubt the "in any way", all I can say is, what a falling off is here, now in later life, from what was in the day of sanguine hopes.'

Of the years he spent at Cambridge little more can be said with certainty, for he made no impact whatever as a scholar and took no part in athletic sports. We know that he read prodigiously but with little sense of purpose and that his defective grounding in the classics prevented him from obtaining more than a pass degree. His first work of fiction was published at this time, by Meadows of Cambridge—*The Chorister. A Tale of King's College Chapel during the Civil Wars*. It only bore his initials and a footnote read: 'For the foundation of the story,

Learning and Teaching

see Treumann's "Historical Notices of Collegiate Building". A very rare book.'

Rare indeed, for no such book ever existed save in Sabine's imagination. He had succeeded in perpetrating one of those complicated hoaxes which were the joy of young Victorians. The chief interest of the book lies in the fact that he must already have developed the power of writing interestingly and convincingly, as it ran to ten editions.

During the long vacations of 1854 and 1855 he continued to ride and tramp over Dartmoor and he grew to know and love it as few then did; a fact that was to prove invaluable to him in later years when, as leader of the Dartmoor Exploration Committee, he was to prepare the first detailed report on its antiquities. He also spent many long, solitary hours in drawing the ancient oak and stone pulpits and rood-screens in its churches, thus acquiring a practical knowledge of church interiors, which was to be of great service to him when, many years later, he restored Lew Trenchard church.

While at Cambridge his already strong religious views crystallised and by 1857 he was an ardent member of the Tractarian Movement. All his natural love of beautiful things, his veneration for the past, all his contempt for what he considered the unspiritual qualities which in his boyhood travels he had grown to associate with continental Lutheranism, led him inevitably into the second wave of the battle that was then raging round the Catholic revival within the Anglican Church.

Like that other West country novelist and cleric, Charles Kingsley, he was a born partisan fighter, but whereas Kingsley, with his deep mistrust of the Roman Church, emphasised only the Protestant side of the Church of England, Sabine's every instinct led him to fight passionately to uphold its Catholic and Apostolic heritage.

It is hard in these days of tolerant indifference to realise the violent passions aroused by religious controversy in England

Learning and Teaching

little more than a century ago. It was against a background of bitter and unreasoning prejudice that the Catholic Revival within the Church of England took place. Evangelical Anglicans united with Nonconformists in an intense mistrust of anyone who by the simplest use of vestments, candles, credence tables or incense seemed to them to be 'flirting with Rome'.

The Church of England was at that time deeply mistrusted by the poor. In rural districts the parson was too often the fool of the family who, under the system of private patronage, was pitchforked into the living by his relative the squire, simply because he was unfit for anything else. In the slums of our nineteenth century cities it was still remembered that the bishops had opposed the great Reform Bill almost to a man.

When he took his degree Sabine's thoughts were already turning to ordination, but his mind was in complete turmoil. He realised that he was out of touch with the workaday world about him. Family tradition was against his taking Holy Orders, for he was the eldest son, the future squire, and the rectory must be reserved for a younger brother. When it came to earning a living he knew his limitations only too well. Though very widely read he had no specialised training that would help him in any profession. To his father's suggestion that he should seek a post at Marlborough Grammar School, where his uncle Frederick Bond was headmaster, he returned a flat refusal. He was in the mood to refuse any suggestion made by his father. One imagines stormy scenes between them for they were both strong-minded men of completely different outlook and character.

Quietly Sabine slipped away and volunteered to teach, not at Marlborough but in the Choir School of St Barnabas, Pimlico. The parish was a theological storm centre, but for him it was a refuge. He had already spent Christmas and Easter vacations there, lodging in Ebury Street and frequenting the church and College, and had been deeply impressed by what he had seen of the work done by its Tractarian clergy. But now he went one

Learning and Teaching

step further and lived as a layman in the clergy-house itself, conforming to its strictly Catholic discipline.

It was here that he met and fell under the influence of the senior curate, the Rev Charles Fuge Lowder, one of the fighting saints of the Tractarian movement. From Pimlico, Lowder went to work in the terrible slums of the London Docks.* The fine work that he and other clergy did in the East End of London and the difficulties and prejudices with which they had to contend were vividly described by Sabine when he came to write his *Reminiscences* and *The Church Revival*. Of the 'disgusting scenes' that took place when organised rioters tried to break up the ritualistic services, he had personal experience while living in Pimlico. Feeling was at this time running very high between the High and Low church parties. 'The clergy,' wrote R. H. Maldon in his book *The English Church and Nation* (1952) 'who were working in large parishes, especially in the more squalid parts of London, felt that they could make very little impression unless they gave their people something to see as well as to hear. More light and colour must be introduced into the Church's worship. Unfortunately these clergy, who were devoted parish priests, seem to have known very little of the principles of religious ceremonial—if during a holiday on the Continent they saw anything which appealed to them, they imitated it at home without much consideration as to its real meaning or intrinsic suitability. This led to violent outbreaks—some of which were deliberately fostered by outsiders!' Sabine was young, impressionable and by nature a partisan. When he saw at first hand something of the violent outbreaks above referred to, at which church services were interrupted and church ornaments overthrown, he was deeply outraged and his whole outlook became prejudiced for life.

Slum conditions in the East End of London at that time were

* cf C. F. Lowder, *Twenty-one years in St George's Mission* (1877) and *Charles Lowder* (1881) M. Tench.

Learning and Teaching

abominable, and produced the orgy of drunkenness, violence, vice and crime only to be expected. Though not one of the worst districts Pimlico was bad enough, for it was ugly, dirty, and poverty-stricken in the extreme. What the effects of such an environment were upon a young man of Sabine's tastes and upbringing we can only guess. He had, it is true, met grinding poverty on the continent when visiting the sick with his mother, but he had never before lived, day in day out, in close contact with it.

Edward Baring-Gould continued to object strongly to what Sabine was doing. Sabine's work in the Choir School was voluntary and unpaid. He received nothing but his board and lodging and after a while he found himself short of even the barest necessities, but his father refused him financial help unless he gave up his way of life, and this he firmly refused to do. Complete deadlock seemed to have been reached. His only contact with his parents at this time was through his grandmother's brother, General Sir Edward Sabine, who lived in London, to whom Sabine was devoted and after whom he had been named. The General, who in his youth had taken part in the voyages of Arctic exploration led by Sir Edward Parry and Sir James Ross, was a distinguished soldier, a scientist and former President of the Royal Society. On one occasion he took his grand-nephew to see an exhibition of the carved bones and other relics of prehistoric man discovered on the Vézère by Christy and Lartet: Sabine was thrilled as he gazed on the pictures of rhinoceros, mammoths and reindeer engraved on the bones and realised something of their implications.

> The whole science of early man was then in its infancy, and the revelations of Lyell, Christy and Lartet and others startled the world, and made the believers in the Textual Infallibility of the Bible, of Creation and Adam and Eve, shake in their shoes.

Page 35: *Sabine, aged 88.*

Sabine in old age: taken about the same time as the Melton Fisher portrait (page 17).

Page 36: *Grace Baring-Gould, wife of Sabine.*

Mary Dickinson (1869-1945), eldest child of Sabine and Grace.

Learning and Teaching

Like Charles Kingsley, who said that he could not believe that God put the fossils in the rocks in order to deceive us, Sabine was too honest not to accept the evidence of evolution, and in years to come was to adapt the theory to the development of religious belief—in a book that was to bring a torrent of abuse upon his head.

For the time he was still deeply unsettled in his ideas and in mental distress. Eventually he confided his troubles to Lowder, who managed to effect a compromise by finding him the post of assistant master, first at the Woodard School, Lancing, and then at Hurstpierpoint, though why he preferred these schools to Marlborough Grammar School it is hard to say, except that it was his father who had suggested Marlborough. He remained at Hurstpierpoint for eight years, working for a salary which began at £25 per year and was finally raised to £40.

We know something of his life as a schoolmaster, not only from his own account in his *Early Reminiscences* but from two surviving descriptions of him written by old boys, one in 1910 and the other in 1924, the year of his death. Also he revisited Hurstpierpoint in 1894 and the College Magazine for June of that year gives the rose-tinted and glowing account of him as a schoolmaster that one would expect from a school magazine on such an occasion. He seems to have been popular with the boys despite his complete lack of interest in games.

Whether he was equally popular with the other members of the staff is less certain, as he was not the type of man to shine in a common-room. In his *Reminiscences* he describes a number of his fellow masters with his usual ironic frankness, but his personal recollections of his teaching days are not mostly of great interest, being made up of the trivial incidents and mishaps common to boarding-school life at any period. A few great names are mentioned. John Keble, founder of the Oxford Movement, after whom Keble College is named, visited Hurstpierpoint while Sabine was there, as did Samuel Wilberforce, the famous Bishop

Learning and Teaching

of Oxford and later of Winchester, and he describes them both.

The young men of a century ago were as addicted to unconventional dress as those of today and no doubt were eyed as disapprovingly by their elders. Sabine and his contemporaries went through a Ruskin-mad phase of dressing-up aesthetically in knee-breeches and stockings, and brown or claret-coloured velvet coats frogged with braid. He also displayed other forms of mild eccentricity more likely to have endeared him to boys, keeping in the school ground a shaggy Icelandic pony called Bottlebrush, which he had saved from a life in the mines. Also he had a tame bat which spent the daylight hours hanging head downwards in the chimney-corner of his study, but which sometimes preferred to cling to his shoulder while he was teaching, 'to the great amusement of the boys and distraction from their lesson' as he himself admits, adding that 'the boys called it my Familiar, and thought that it whispered strange secrets in my ear'. Just what the headmaster thought of it all we are not told, but he probably had the good sense to turn a blind eye, knowing that in Sabine he had a first-class linguist and teacher.

> One day the head master, Dr Lowe, sent me to his German class. I was staggered. I had not spoken a word of German or read a German book since 1844 and fifteen years had elapsed; after leaving Deutschland I had been so much in France that I had come to talk and think in French. To my surprise I found the language came back to me with a rush, and as at that time I was learning Icelandic and had only an Icelandic grammar in German, I again read the language.

Above all 'Snout', to give him his nickname, was long remembered as a story-teller. The type of yarn that he told his pupils on winter evenings in his study, or during the long walks that he took with them on half-holidays, can be gauged by the following extract from the preface of his *Grettir the Outlaw*, published

Learning and Teaching

some thirty years later. It also gives us a glimpse of that extraordinary capacity for work, which throughout his life, was perhaps his most remarkable characteristic:

> It is now just thirty years since I first began to read the 'Saga of Grettir the Strong' in Icelandic. At that time I had only a Danish Grammar of Icelandic and an Icelandic-Danish Dictionary, and I did not know a word of Danish. . . . But after I had worked a little way into the Saga, I became intensely interested in it myself, and it struck me that my boys whom I taught might like to hear about Grettir. So I tried every day to translate, after school hours, a chapter, hardly ever more at first, and sometimes not even as much as that. Then, when on half-holidays I proposed a walk to some of my scholars, they were keen to hear the story of Grettir. Well, Grettir went on for some months in this way, a fresh instalment of the tale coming every half-holiday, and it was really wonderful how interested and delighted the boys were in the story.

The voice of a dedicated and gifted teacher is apparent, but the two accounts quoted above also contain a revealing little detail which is characteristic of the man: in the preface to *Grettir the Outlaw*, written some thirty years after the event that he is describing, he mentions that it was from a Danish-Icelandic dictionary that he taught himself Icelandic. In the quotation from his *Early Reminiscences*, written some thirty years after that, it was a German-Icelandic dictionary.

Especially towards the end of his life, Sabine depended far too much on a remarkable but failing memory.

While at Hurstpierpoint he must have been at least partly reconciled to his father and have received some allowance from the Lew Trenchard estate, of which he was now heir, or he could hardly have indulged in a remarkable holiday trip to Iceland in 1861, which proved to be something of a saga in itself. Iceland was still inaccessible and almost unknown to the world at large. Living conditions were primitive and exploration had to be made

Learning and Teaching

on foot or pony-back. *Iceland, its Scenes and Sagas*, was one of the best travel books he ever wrote, and one which has the additional interest of being illustrated by a number of his own sketches, made on the spot. It was during the return voyage from Iceland that Sabine strained his eyes badly by continuous reading in a cabin lit only by a swaying lantern. From that time onwards his sight continued to deteriorate until in old age he was half blind.

All his life the Norse sagas, the Germanic legends and, incidentally, Wagner's music, were to have for Sabine a deep fascination. Beneath the surface of his genuinely spiritual nature, and often in conflict with it, lay strange depths that drew him to those dark byways that underlie all folklore. One imagines that his pupils were at times delightfully horrified, during the winter evening sessions in his study, by strange legends of trolls, vampires and werewolves. Certainly this macabre tendency was deeply ingrained in his nature, though only in *Mehalah*, his one novel with any real claim to greatness, did it ever come completely to the surface.

One of the few things that Edward and Sabine Baring-Gould held in common were their political convictions. Edward we know on Sabine's authority to have been a 'strong Whig'; it was he, not Sabine, who once wrote:

> Look at our hunting and sporting gentry; you see what their legs and arms are about, whether riding after hounds or striding after partridges and pheasants, but their heads—they are stagnant pools in which there is no mental circulation. I do not reproach them. God made them so, but I do not care for their society.

Sabine was a 'Zealous Radical' in his teaching days and although he later toned down, as he himself put it, he remained all his life a staunch Liberal. He concurred entirely with his father's

Learning and Teaching

attitude of amused contempt for the activities of many of the sporting squires, who were his neighbours in Lew Trenchard during the last forty years of his life, and many years later he quoted Edward's remarks with obvious glee—though his feelings never prevented him from accepting gifts of game.

I

The Curate of Horbury Brig

That Sabine, left to himself, would have sought ordination long before he was thirty years of age there can be no doubt. He was obviously contemplating it as early as the days of the 'Holy Club'. It is hard today to understand the violent family opposition that he had to face and overcome, or for that matter the fact that he felt it absolutely necessary to do so before taking the plunge. That not only his dictatorial, strong-willed father, but also his mother, strongly disapproved of the idea seems all the more remarkable as Mrs Baring-Gould was a deeply religious woman, who had been brought up in the old, traditional church principles, which she practised with great regularity all her life, never failing to say her short 'Office' of prayer seven times every day. Sabine might well have expected her to encourage him in his desire for ordination, but in fact she only withdrew her opposition shortly before her death from cancer in 1863. It was not until both his brothers had, on growing to manhood, refused to comply with the unwritten rule that the squire must always have a younger brother available to fill the family living when it became vacant, that his father at last gave his reluctant consent.

The final step was taken in an extraordinarily haphazard

The Curate of Horbury Brig

manner, for Sabine offered himself as assistant curate to the Rev John Sharp, Rector of Horbury in Yorkshire, simply to allow another man, who would have gone there, to come instead to Hurstpierpoint as chaplain.

If Sabine's confirmation had been unimpressive, his ordination by Robert Bickersteth, the evangelical Bishop of Ripon, was even more so. As a young man, Sabine had been described as having a singularly sweet face but, sweet-faced or not, he had at times a most acid pen, which he used unsparingly, especially when writing about his ecclesiastical superiors. Of his ordination he wrote:

> Accordingly I took an early train and called on the Bishop at the hour appointed, when he had just finished his breakfast; and he came in to see me, wiping some egg from his lips, and a drop from his black silk apron. . . . He received me stiffly, being more interested in getting the drop of egg off his apron than in enquiring into my qualifications.

He then goes on to describe the examining chaplain as having a face that would have qualified him for the Chamber of Horrors at Mme Tussaud's waxworks. On this occasion at least he must have succeeded in keeping his thoughts sufficiently to himself to pass muster, for he was ordained 'in a black gown, no cassock', on Whitsunday 1864, not in the cathedral, but in the chapel of the palace.

The following day, without further preparation of any sort, he arrived at Horbury to begin his new life. Anyone watching at the station that day would have seen a tall, good-looking, correctly dressed clergyman stepping off the train, carrying draped over his shoulders a long black bag containing his luggage. He must have presented a curious appearance, for the bag was so long that it nearly touched the ground on either side of him as he walked. 'Gould's black slug', as the Hurstpierpoint boys had named this object, was already famous. It dated from

The Curate of Horbury Brig

his Icelandic expedition and had been designed by him for strapping across a pony's back when riding over rough country. It is characteristic of the man that he had used it ever since with a complete disregard for the oddity of its appearance.

Fortunately for Sabine he was to serve his first and only curacy under the Rev John Sharp, a hard and devoted worker of great experience, who had the rare good sense to guide without attempting to rule his unusual thirty-year-old curate. Had he been the fussy, autocratic parish priest, obsessed with his own self-importance, the results would almost certainly have proved disastrous. Instead he realised that his assistant was not a boy but an experienced schoolmaster, used to taking responsibility; a man not only capable of working alone, but one who was temperamentally best suited to do so. Almost at once he gave Sabine a section of the parish to look after by himself and never interfered with the work there in any way. The result very soon proved his wisdom. The section of the parish in which Sabine was entrusted with the task of developing a mission was known as Horbury Brig. It had all the rough, roaring vigour of its type and period. In some ways it resembled the pioneer towns of Western America more than any place we could find in England today. The population consisted of canal boatmen, colliers and mill workers, who fought, gambled and drank prodigiously. Every man had his whippet for rabbit coursing or his game-cock for cock fighting; most were illiterate and few if any took the slightest interest in religion. Among them strode the tall, frock-coated clergyman, and somehow, almost from the first, he began to win their respect and affection. His experience as a schoolmaster led him to start at the right end with the young people, and by winning them over he gained a number of their parents as well. He found that his previous experience as a teacher and teller of stories proved to be a tremendous asset in his new task. Renting a small cottage, he opened the ground floor as a night school. The bedroom above became a chapel, the chimney-piece

The Curate of Horbury Brig

serving as altar with cross and candles upon it. When Sabine stood upon the stool which did duty as pulpit, his head touched the ceiling. The cross that stood on this improvised altar at Horbury Brig is still in existence. In 1961, a dilapidated Paschal Cross made of carved and painted wood was found in Lew Trenchard church. Sabine's grandson repaired it and six years later he chanced on the fact that Sabine had referred, in a hitherto unpublished manuscript, to just such a cross in Lew Trenchard church, as having been bought by him while still at Cambridge and used in Horbury Brig.

Every Sunday evening Sabine held services, and the congregation soon filled both the chapel and the schoolroom downstairs; the resulting time-lag, between the upstairs and downstairs portions of the congregation, producing curious results during the hymn-singing. Sabine at thirty had abundant zeal and tremendous energy, but above all he had splendid material on which to work. In days of compulsory free education for all it is only too easy to forget the pathetic, desperate yearning of the illiterate for the rudiments of scholarship, but that it existed there can be no shadow of doubt. In consequence, Sabine's night-school proved a great success. There was, it is true, a certain amount of opposition at first from that rowdy element that always exists, but it soon died away.

The young people loved the school and they clearly loved their teacher. When lessons were ended he was always expected to tell some story before the class dismissed. 'The boys and girls,' wrote an old pupil, 'used to get on Baring-Gould's coat-laps to keep him prisoner, and sing out in chorus, "You mun tell us a tale afore you go." Then he would begin, "Once upon a time" and he made it up as he went along and it always suited us.'

So successful was the mission that it soon filled almost all Sabine's time and his connection with the parish church grew steadily less. It was not long before the cottage became far too small and had to be replaced by a larger building. The stone for this was provided free by a local quarry owner, Mr Knowles, who from the start had helped Sabine in every possible way. John Sharp pleaded for the mission among his friends and admirers. Sabine wrote an appeal to the *Church Times* and also pestered his friends and relations for help. The people of the district, though mostly poor, gave generously. Sometimes contributions came from unexpected sources: ten shillings was sent by a man whose dog had won a wager for him by killing a rival dog in a set fight one Sunday morning.

Within two years of Sabine's arrival in Horbury Brig, a new stone-built school-chapel had been opened, free from debt. Always a man of unusual physical strength and energy, Sabine was at that time in the prime of life, but at Horbury Brig he drove himself to the limit. By the end of the day he was often too weary to walk back to the rectory and would pass the night in an armchair in the cottage. Yet in addition to all his other work at the mission, he somehow found time to write. Page after page was covered in his minute, tidy handwriting. Much of what he then wrote has long been forgotten, but two of his most famous hymns date from this period, 'On the Resurrection Morning' and 'Onward, Christian Soldiers'.

Both these hymns attained world-wide and lasting fame, and like so much else that he wrote, both created plenty of controversy. It is the fashion to question the theology of the former, though it has certainly brought comfort to a number of bereaved persons including, it is said, Queen Victoria. 'Onward, Christian Soldiers' has been constantly attacked for a number of reasons, but it still goes on being sung: with 'Abide with me' it has in fact become the best-known hymn in the English language. To the Evangelicals of his day it seemed dangerously ritualistic and to extreme Protestants it was anathema. In his old age, however, Sabine denied the authenticity of the much-quoted story that when an Evangelical Bishop of Exeter objected to the line 'With the Cross of Jesus going on before' he had sarcastically offered to

The Curate of Horbury Brig

substitute 'With the Cross of Jesus left behind the door'. 'The story,' wrote Sabine in 1918, 'was invented by my eldest son, when an American interviewer called on him in New York for some copy about the hymn'. But there seems to have been at least some foundation for the tale—one not out of keeping with Sabine's gift of irony and lifelong contempt for authority—for Sabine himself wrote in his *Further Reminiscences*:

> Bickersteth [E. H. Bickersteth, Bishop of Exeter] was a kind amiable man, but very vain over his 'poems' in which are no poetical ideas, and his hymnal that has almost everywhere been superseded.
> He wanted to alter my 'Onward, Christian Soldiers' in the line 'With the Cross of Jesus going on before' into 'With our Lord and Master going on before' or some twaddle like it.

'Onward, Christian Soldiers' was probably written in 1864, and first sung at a children's Whitsunday procession at Horbury Brig in 1865. Originally set to a tune by Haydn, it undoubtedly owes much of its lasting popularity to Sullivan's setting, to which it is universally sung. The words first appeared in the *Church Times* in 1864, but in his old age Sabine obviously associated it in his mind with his Horbury Brig Mission and spoke of it as though it had been especially written for the children's procession in 1865; an easy slip for an old man to make.

The hymn has been sung on many great occasions, including the second World War meeting between Winston Churchill and President Roosevelt on board ship, when the Atlantic Charter was agreed upon. Its vitality survived all Evangelical prejudice and its popularity continues: it is to be found even in the *Methodist Hymn Book*, complete with 'the cross of Jesus going on before'. It is still of course severely criticised, as by William Purcell in his book *Onward, Christian Soldier*: 'Confidently, almost stridently urging others along, it yet enshrines no spiritual experience, and for that reason alone it might well be judged shallow, extrovert, dangerously open to ridicule.'

In 1916, during the first World War, Sabine's daughter Mary listened in London to a sermon which attacked the hymn on the grounds that the Church of God, far from being a mighty army, was nothing but an undisciplined rabble. She duly chaffed her father about this, but the old man was not to be drawn. He probably agreed with the preacher, for his own outlook had changed greatly since the hymn was first written, as the following letter clearly shows:

Lew Trenchard,
Lew Down.
Ascension Day.
1912.

My very dear Mary,

Thank you so much for the delightful photograph of yourself which I found awaiting me on my return to Lew yesterday. And oh! I was so glad to be home again. I was not well all the time I was in Exeter, bronchitis as usual, but this spell of hot weather has set me up again.

Some char-a-bancs from Bude, packed with Methodies and their minister are arriving this morning to see the church, grounds and house. I hope they will not depart singing 'We are not divided, all One Body We' for it would be a lie.

I remain
with renewed thanks
yrs ever sincerely
S. Baring-Gould.

All his four hymns; 'Onward, Christian Soldiers', 'On the Resurrection Morning', 'Through the Night of Doubt and Sorrow', and 'Now the Day is Over' were written while he was at Horbury. Autographed copies of them were presented to the **Dean and Chapter of Exeter Cathedral by Sir Leicester Harms-**

The Curate of Horbury Brig

worth and Mr H. C. Harmsworth, and were to be seen there in a case in the south aisle, prior to the second World War, but they were destroyed during the bombing of the city on the night of 3 May 1942. There must be, scattered about the world, a large number of holograph copies of Sabine's hymns, for at one time in his later life an enterprising American dealer offered him a dollar each for any copies that he cared to write out, and he would often come down to breakfast chuckling that, old as he was, he had earned a pound before anyone else in the house was awake.

The controversy round 'Onward, Christian Soldiers' still goes on. As recently as 19 November 1963, Mr Lionel Dakers, organist to Exeter Cathedral, when addressing the Diocesan Conference on the subject of Church music, said:

> Much of the nineteenth century music is justly accused of being Victorian in the worst sense of the term, for it employs cloying sentiment and does little or nothing to present a positive picture of the Church today as being something strong and vital. One of the few exceptions is, strangely, 'Onward, Christian Soldiers', yet we take for granted and often without much thought, the strength of Baring-Gould's magnificent words. They are inseparably allied to a tune of doubtful musical value, but one which has many sentimental associations, yet the words form the kernel of what the Church is striving to achieve today in unity.

Despite its detractors the hymn is still very much alive and to celebrate its centenary in 1965 it was sung processionally by Sunday School children in many parts of England.

Today the main objectors to it are pacifically minded people who dislike singing anything so warlike; but then the hymn is, as Ian Hay once said, one of the few real warsongs of the Church Militant, and that surely is what Sabine intended it to be. One verse is, however, invariably omitted today, and is not in any

The Curate of Horbury Brig

of the standard hymnals: the original fourth verse formed a link between the third and fifth verses. It ran as follows:

> What the saints established
> That I hold for true,
> What the saints believed
> That believe I too;
> Long as earth endureth
> Men that faith will hold,
> Kingdoms, nations, empires
> In destruction rolled.

The title is now part of our language and in 1964, the centenary of its first appearance in the *Church Times*, a book by Diana Dewar, dealing with the impact of religious teaching on young children, was published under the title *Backward Christian Soldiers*. With much that this book contained Sabine would undoubtedly have been in complete agreement and some of it he anticipated many years ago in his own writing and preaching.

4

Dalton i't Muck

From the virile, noisy life at Horbury Brig, Sabine moved in 1867 to the obscure little parish of Dalton, commonly known as 'Dalton i't Muck', in the East Riding of Yorkshire. A greater change would be hard to imagine, for Dalton was an entirely agricultural parish of less than one hundred inhabitants. It was in fact at that time scarcely worthy of the name of parish, for it had only a short while before been cut out of the large parish of Topcliffe, by the efforts of the Dowager Viscountess Downe, who owned most of the land in the district. During the lifetime of her husband, Topcliffe had been divided to form three parishes, Topcliffe, Sessay and Baldersby, and soon after his death his widow decided that Dalton should form yet a fourth.

Lord Downe had been a progressive landlord and had worked hard to improve the estate. At Sessay he had built a new church and constructed a number of well-built cottages for his tenants. At Baldersby he had done even more. Not only a new church, but school-buildings, a vicarage and a number of cottages had been built. But when Sabine went to Dalton it was still very neglected. A large barn served the dual purpose of church and school and the vicarage was a small red-brick building with only

Dalton i't Muck

one sitting-room, kitchen and scullery on the ground floor.

From the start Sabine found himself in difficulties. For one thing he soon discovered that his new parishioners were very different from the eager, active-minded people of Horbury Brig. They were slower and less intelligent and he was one who temperamentally found stupidity hard to bear. The religious life of the parish, such as it was, also presented him with problems. At Horbury he had to start from scratch and had had on the whole a wonderful response, but at Dalton he had been preceded by an extreme High Churchman, who rejoiced in excessive ritualism to the complete bewilderment of his congregation. Tractarian though he was, Sabine had the practical common sense to realise the stupidity of conducting services in this manner in a rural area. He simplified the ritual as much as he could without making too violent a break with previous practice there.

But it was Viscountess Downe, acting patron of the living and owner of every house in the parish, who constituted his greatest problem. He gives us a detailed and, for him, not unkindly picture of her in his *Reminiscences*. She belonged to an order and a way of life that was, even then, rapidly disintegrating. Towards her tenantry she had a strong sense of responsibility and looked after the sick and aged among them with meticulous care. But she demanded in return a complete submission to her will from everyone about her, including the parson, whom she had appointed, and whom she treated as a sort of superior servant, to be rewarded with gifts of game and fruit from 'The Park' should he please her by complying with her wishes in every detail, even down to the choice of hymns and the length of the Sunday sermon.

Sabine's predecessor had slavishly conformed to her orders, doing nothing without first consulting her, and had in consequence been much in favour, but Sabine proved less amenable, even at times daring openly to oppose her. Nor was he the only rebel. The rector of Baldersby told him that he simply could not

Page 53: (above and below) *Lew Trenchard Church, the parish church of St Peter, as it stands today.* 'Peravi lucernam Christo meo'.

Page 54: (above) *Lew House (Lew Trenchard Hotel) as it is today;* (below) *the Lew Trenchard Menhir. This stone was discovered by Sabine Baring-Gould during repairs to Lew Mill. He had it removed from the side of the mill-leat and erected it on its proper site in front of the mill.*

Dalton i't Muck

remain in such close proximity to the Park and keep his self-respect, and that a former rector had been forced by Lady Downe to resign his living because he had dared to show that he had a mind of his own. There was little or no social life, nor much chance of congenial intellectual companionship for a man of Sabine's tastes and interests. With his fellow clergy of the deanery he soon found that he had nothing in common and while at Dalton he only troubled to attend one ruridecanal meeting—of which, fifty years later, he gave an ironic pen-picture in his *Further Reminiscences*.

One thing only is certain and that is that he was never really happy or at home in Dalton. Why then had he left Horbury Brig, where he had done good work and where his energies were fully engaged? The one possible answer is that his approaching marriage to Grace Taylor of Horbury Brig made a move advisable and that he took the first chance that offered itself.

The story of his courtship and marriage is an extraordinary one, the details of which can never now be fully known. His *Reminiscences*, as published posthumously, merely mention that he married Miss Grace Taylor of Horbury on 28 May 1868, but he did tell the whole story in a passage that has mysteriously vanished (see chapter 13). To realise all that their marriage implied one must remember the rigidity of the social barriers of that time.

An amusing, if apocryphal, story is told by Conan Doyle of a peer living in Regency days who doubled his son's allowance when he ran off with the cook, saying that it was the first glimmer of intelligence that the young man had ever displayed, but it would be hard to imagine a mid-Victorian father doing the same. Perhaps to bolster their obstinate refusal to admit the upheaval taking place in the world around them, the survivors of the 'ruling few' were clinging more closely to their tattered social prestige than at any other period of English history. Sabine was the eldest son of a 'county' family; Grace Taylor, when he

Dalton i't Muck

first met her, was a mill-girl of sixteen. She had begun work at the age of ten; her parents were poor and she herself was practically illiterate. How they first met is not known: it may have been at Sabine's night-school, or while he was visiting her sick mother. But with this beautiful, unsophisticated child, the severe, scholarly clergyman of over thirty fell desperately, passionately in love. The storm of opposition and gossip that their wooing must have aroused in all quarters can be guessed, but in 1866 they became engaged and it was in the following year that Sabine left Horbury for Dalton.

It has been assumed that when in his first novel, *Through Flood and Flame*, published in the same year as his marriage, Sabine told the story of the love of a clergyman's son for a poor mill-girl, he was drawing largely upon memories of his own courtship. An indication of the autobiographical nature of the novel is that the young man sends the girl to be educated by a relative of his vicar; and this is precisely what Sabine did with Grace. Sabine's eldest daughter, Mary, always said that it was John Sharp who befriended the lovers and that it was to a lady relative of his that Grace was sent to be educated. This is almost certainly correct, for Mary was not only far more in her parents' confidence than were her younger brothers and sisters, but kept in touch with her Taylor relations all her life. That at the time not only the Baring-Goulds but the Taylors were bitterly opposed to the marriage may be gathered from the fact that no member of either family was present at the wedding, which took place very quietly after Matins in front of two members of the congregation who had been asked to remain as witnesses. A short honeymoon on the Continent followed—during which, incidentally, Sabine bought the fine picture of the Crucifixion by Lavidière which now hangs in Lew Trenchard church. This was a characteristic action, for throughout his life the chief value of money for him was that it allowed him to surround himself with beautiful things.

Dalton i't Muck

The little mill-girl in *Through Flood and Flame* is made to speak in a Yorkshire dialect and if this is really a portrait of Grace in girlhood the transformation made by those two years was remarkable, for no one who remembers her can recall even a trace of Yorkshire accent. She was to emerge as a quietly self-possessed clergyman's wife, the much-loved mother of an ever-increasing family (in all she was to bear Sabine fifteen children), and finally as the gentle, dignified Lady of the Manor of Lew Trenchard. Nor was this all. For the greater part of his life, Sabine was to be a controversial and picturesque figure, but to those who knew her personally, Grace was never in any way overshadowed by the formidable figure of her husband. It is true that her enormous family prevented her from taking part in local social life as much as she might otherwise have done. For much of her married life she was either expecting another baby or recovering from a recent confinement, and in her last years she became an invalid and was finally bedridden; but her restraining influence and shrewd Yorkshire common sense played a far greater part in Sabine's life than the outside world, or even the younger members of his own family, ever guessed. Probably no one but Mary ever fully realised how great and how beneficial her influence on Sabine was. During his long and active life, Sabine's impulsive nature and scathing pen earned him enemies, and without Grace they would have earned him many more. Again and again he would impetuously dash off a biting letter and show it to her. She would read it through carefully: 'Yes, dear,' she would say, 'but don't post it till tomorrow', knowing perfectly well that by the following morning he would have cooled off sufficiently not to post it at all.

Grace was still only eighteen when she assumed the role of vicar's wife. Life in the isolated vicarage must have required extensive readjustment from a girl brought up in the noisy good-fellowship of an industrial town. For entertainment Sabine would read to her as she worked in the kitchen, choosing, we are told, such books as Motley's *Revolt in the Netherlands*, by which he presumably meant *The Rise of the Dutch Republic*. Grace was very much in love with him, but one cannot help wondering what she really thought of his choice of light reading. She always retained a strong taste for the gay things of life and many years later, when she paid a visit to her eldest son Edward in London, she made it quite clear on arrival that she wished to be taken to the theatre to see not the Shakespeare play which Sabine had thoughtfully suggested for her, but a gay, fast-moving revue of the type then beginning to become popular. It was not in fact until their eldest daughter Mary began to grow up that Sabine found a companion whose love of serious reading equalled his own.

Sabine can never have been an easy man to live with. He was quick-tempered, impatient, and when engaged on writing a book, as he nearly always was, apt to become completely absent-minded. On one occasion, when asked by Grace to buy some meat for dinner, he allowed the butcher to sell him a forty-pound joint of beef. Once purchased it had to be eaten, and the two of them struggled with it till they were weary of the sight of beef, cold, curried and rehashed. Only by asking the choir boys to supper were they finally rid of it. The story may be amusing in retrospect, but that sort of unpracticality cannot have made it easier to battle with the problems of housekeeping on a limited income. And though a capable amateur artist, Sabine was no handyman. His curious upbringing had denied him even those normal boyish hobbies that involve the use of tools. When he did attempt to be practical the results were apt to be disastrous. When on one occasion he made a desperate attempt to repaper the mouldering vicarage, his complete incompetence reduced him to such a raging fury that the terrified Grace fled back to Horbury to consult the long-suffering John Sharp and beg him to unmarry them.

For how long they might have been bogged down at Dalton

Dalton i't Muck

it is difficult to say, but for one event that made possible a new chapter in their lives. Frustrated in his parish work, Sabine, to whom inactivity was torment, had turned his energies more and more to writing. One of his earliest books to be published while he was at Dalton was *The Silver Store*, a collection of versified legends drawn from the medieval, Christian and Jewish sources, which with unusual tact he dedicated to the Dowager Viscountess Downe. Far from any good library, Sabine must have depended on his extraordinarily encyclopaedic mind for most of his information. He had a highly developed photographic memory. Many years later he told his son-in-law, Harvey Dickinson, that he could read off in his mind any page of any book that had ever interested him. A few men do have this phenomenal gift, but for the scholar it holds dangers. There is no doubt that Sabine grew to depend on it far too much and his work suffered in consequence. In later life particularly, the storehouse of his mind became an unreliable lumber room, especially where dates and measurements were concerned. When he was at Dalton, however, he was at the zenith of his mental powers and the weakness had not shown itself.

Among the many books that he wrote at this time was the two-volume work on *The Origin and Development of Religious Belief*. To a modern reader it would seem mild, and much of it is indeed completely outdated; but for its period it was an original, bold and controversial book, certain to produce heated controversy, bound to disturb strictly orthodox Christians. The leaders of the Christian Church have seldom shown at their best when confronted by new ideas. It is not the parson's fault that he so seldom shines in debate, for his whole training and way of life tend to unfit him for the quick cut and thrust of verbal argument with intellectual equals. He is a trained public speaker, often a good one, but he has had no real training in debate. If he sits on a public platform and tries to argue his case, his opponent is usually as well educated as himself and far more

Dalton i't Muck

experienced in argument. The majority of his listeners automatically assume that the better advocate has the better case. Though modern media of mass-communication have emphasised this fact, there is nothing new in it. In 1860, orthodox Christians were deeply disturbed when the silver-tongued Samuel Wilberforce, then Bishop of Oxford, constituted himself the champion of the Book of Genesis and attacked Professor Huxley at a meeting of the Royal Society.

Wilberforce was a man of considerable ability and oratorical powers. He had for many years been famous as a preacher, but opposed to the clear reasoning mind of the great scientist, the bishop's professional eloquence sounded thin indeed. The whole audience felt that religion had crossed swords with science and that religion had lost the day. So great was the emotional tension that one woman in the audience actually fainted.

Now, a decade later, an obscure country clergyman called Baring-Gould was apparently trying to prove that religious belief itself must evolve, as man grew to live differently and think differently. The response was immediate. Roman Catholics, High Anglicans and extreme Protestants for once combined in their condemnation of the book and its author. Of all the controversies, and they were many, that Sabine's writings provoked, this was perhaps the most bitter and long lasting. Fortunately for Sabine no less a person than Gladstone, at that time Prime Minister, read the book and was sufficiently impressed despite the popular outcry, to offer the author the Crown living of East Mersea in Essex, which happened to be vacant.

To Sabine this meant escape. Thankfully, in 1871, he transferred himself and his family from the muck of Dalton to the mud-flats of the Essex coast, and there he remained for the next ten years.

5

The Rector of East Mersea

In 1872, the year after Sabine's arrival in East Mersea, Edward Baring-Gould died, and Sabine, as his eldest son, inherited the Lew Trenchard estate. For a number of reasons, some of which were undoubtedly financial, he decided to remain for a time at least in Essex.

Among the many puzzles that surround his life, his financial position is one of the hardest to solve. It will be necessary to return to this more fully later, for it has a considerable bearing on what followed, but for the moment it suffices to say that Sabine himself, with his mental blindness where figures were concerned, never really found a satisfactory answer to it. As a beneficed clergyman he had his stipend, such as it was. His huge output of books must have brought him in a considerable income, for though his theological writings never had more than a limited circulation, his novels had at one time a large reading public. But the Lew Trenchard estate was, for reasons to be related later, more often a liability than a financial asset. Already, when he inherited it, the abolition of the Corn Laws had greatly changed the pattern of English farming, although the real period of agricultural depression did not commence for another decade.

The Rector of East Mersea

As head of the family, too, Sabine found that he now had greatly increased responsibilities. These included his younger brother William, who was adored by his parents and liked by all who had not lent him money. He had depended on his father during Edward's lifetime and now considered it his elder brother's duty to support him. This may not have been altogether William's fault. In youth he had shown a certain talent for engineering, which greatly endeared him to his machine-worshipping father, but he suffered some form of breakdown and from then on did no work of any sort. Whatever the reason, Sabine accepted the necessity to support him. In addition, Edward had married a second time in 1865 and Sabine was now responsible for his step-mother and her two children. His half-brother Arthur was a little boy of seven at the time of their father's death, and his half-sister Lilah, was only three years old, the same age as his own Mary. Nor was this all. His uncle Charles Baring-Gould had been rector of Lew Trenchard since 1832 and remained so until his death in 1881. For the last fourteen years of his life the old man had been ailing, and most of the work of the parish had been entrusted to a succession of curates, whose salaries appear to have been paid by the Baring-Goulds.

So for a number of reasons the new squire of Lew Trenchard remained in East Mersea for another nine years, although he never felt at home there, nor did he get on well with the local people, as he frankly admitted. East Mersea appealed to Sabine as little as did its people and he gives a grim enough picture of it.

> Mersea is an island about three miles long between the mouths of the Blackwater and the Colne. Between it and the mainland is a causeway that is overflowed at high tides. . . . The island is extended seaward by mud-flats for a mile, over which the tide flows. Towards the island the clay has been dug out to form a sea-wall on the land side, leaving a channel between the fields and the flats, and this channel is filled with decaying marine vegetable and animal matter, producing an intolerable stench

The Rector of East Mersea

that pervades the air when the tide goes out and forms a breeding place for myriads of mosquitoes.

He also bewailed its inaccessibility, the lack of company, and the shocking state of the roads in winter owing to the lack of local stone.

For exercise and for reasons of economy, Sabine tended his garden and personally looked after and milked the flock of goats that he had perforce to keep, as cow's milk for his family was not easy to obtain. The eldest children (Mary was twelve before the Baring-Goulds left East Mersea) shared their father's dislike of the place. In particular they grew to hate the long, muddy road along which their daily exercise had to be taken. The only break for them in the monotony of the walk was to rush wildly past a dark and sinister ditch in which they were convinced lurked a kelpie, a malignant water-spirit who drowned and ate unwary passers-by; it appears that Sabine still indulged his taste for folklore when telling stories to his children. In addition, the biting east winds, howling in winter over the sodden mud-flats, brought on a return of the lung trouble from which Sabine had suffered in boyhood. Thrown back upon himself, he spent more and more time in his study, writing continuously, hour after hour.

Meanwhile, year by year, their family continued to increase. Mary, the eldest child, was born in 1869: Margaret (Daisy), in 1870; both at Dalton. The eldest son, Edward, was born in 1871; the next child, Beatrice, was born in 1874, but died in infancy. In 1875 she was followed by another daughter, Veronica; in 1877, a second son, Julian, was born, and he was followed in 1878 by another son, William Drake, and in 1880 by another daughter, Barbara. Thus when they finally left East Mersea in 1881 the Baring-Goulds already had seven children. In the years that followed their last move to Lew Trenchard this number was doubled: Diana Amelia was born in 1882; Felicitas in 1883;

The Rector of East Mersea

Henry in 1885; Joan in 1887; Cicely in 1889; John Hilary in 1890; and finally Grace arrived in 1891 to complete the enormous family. Mary married in the same year as her youngest sister was born, and Sabine's first grandson, Arscott Dickinson, was born two years later.

In due course all Sabine's daughters and all his sons except Henry were to marry and have children, as also were his half-brother Arthur and his half-sister Lilah. It is consequently small wonder that in extreme old age Sabine sometimes failed to recognise his own flesh and blood.

Among the many books that Sabine wrote while at East Mersea, two may be selected as showing something of the strange complexity of his character. The first is his one really first-class novel, *Mehalah*. Though almost forgotten until recently it was at once recognised as an outstanding work of fiction. Besides *Through Flood and Flame* already mentioned, Sabine had written a now forgotten novel of the French Revolution called *In Exitu Israel*, which had been published by Macmillan in 1870, and he had translated a German novel called *Ernestine*, neither of which had attracted much attention. But the publication of *Mehalah* in 1880 placed its writer, almost at one leap, among the leading novelists of his day. It not only met with popular acclaim but greatly admired by men of letters; no less a person than Swinburne comparing it favourably with *Wuthering Heights*. One is inclined to wonder if it might not also have become a classic had it not later been buried beneath a mound of inferior work. Between 1880 and 1906 fourteen impressions of the book were sold out and in 1920 a cheap edition was published by John Murray. Now it is again in print.

Yet it is an extraordinary book to have come from the pen of a Victorian parson and one-time member of the Cambridge Holy Club, for it has about it a brutality, a savagery, seldom equalled in contemporary literature. The scene of this remarkable story of hatred, violence and passion is set amid the wind-swept salt-

The Rector of East Mersea

marshes of the Essex coast, where Sabine was then living, and both the characters and the landscape are vividly and cruelly portrayed. Sabine was indeed a many-sided man, and *Mehalah* seems to have welled up from that deeply buried primitive strain in his character, which drew him irresistibly to the grim Icelandic sagas and the dark underside of Teutonic folklore, and which may have been brought to the surface by the uncongenial nature of the district in which he lived. *Mehalah* may also have been a subconscious reaction against the work that had occupied much of his time and thoughts for several years previously. Between 1872 and 1877 he had produced his monumental *Lives of the Saints* at an agreed rate of one volume every six months. This colossal work contains in all 3,600 saintly biographies, arranged in no sort of chronological or alphabetical order, but according to their traditional Saints' Days. A number of the stories are fascinating; some would be considered by most readers to belong rather to the realm of folklore than history; but one's first reaction on examining the closely packed volumes is amazement at the tremendous expenditure of time and energy devoted to the subject. Originally published in fifteen volumes, another sixteen-volume edition was brought out in 1897-8, and a third, also in sixteen volumes, in 1914.

Wherever did a country clergyman obtain all this mass of information? Where, for that matter, did he have access to the scholar's library essential for its compilation? To what extent did he neglect his work as a parish priest for the sake of this self-imposed task? How did he draw the line, which he knew to exist, between myth and history? For though he included names of dubious historical value, he was well aware that he would be blamed in some quarters for leaving out others enshrined in the old martyrologies.

The whole vast, ramshackle effort was unquestionably an act of piety, for it brought him little financial reward. He never received more than £50 a volume and even this was not always forthcoming, as his publisher, Hodges, became bankrupt during the period of publication. Just how hard the labour proved can be judged by the fact that for the only time in his life he admits in his *Reminiscences* to feeling very tired by the time *The Lives of the Saints* was finished. But the most amazing thing about the book is simply that it was written by the author of *Mehalah*.

At that time Sabine spent considerable periods in London, for in addition to the *Lives of the Saints* he was engaged on a family history that involved much delving among wills in Somerset House. How much, or how little, he saw of his parishioners one cannot say. Sabine's absences were made possible by the fact that he had a great friend, the Rev J. M. Gatrill, in whose charge he would at times leave the parish and who on other occasions accompanied him on those Continental excursions, which again began to form part of his life. Gatrill was a quiet, kindly little man, much beloved by Sabine's elder children. He trailed along behind the dynamic Sabine like a small truck behind a powerful and erratic locomotive. How Gatrill ever found time for all this one cannot imagine: he must have had a singularly obliging vicar, for he is referred to as working as a curate in Leeds.

Twice during these years we hear of Sabine visiting Lew Trenchard. In 1876 his uncle, Charles Baring-Gould, then a feeble old man, begged him to come and put an end to a scandal which was disturbing the peace of the village. After his father's death Sabine had let Lew House. 'The tenant to whom I let Lew House,' he wrote later, 'proved most unsatisfactory. He himself was a poor, blanched creature, like sea-kale but not so tall, and was in fragile health. His wife was a buxom woman. She filled the house with young men, who drank, gambled and flirted with her.

'When a party came to church, it was to behave with so great impropriety as to scandalise the congregation.

'Accordingly I had to give Mr X notice to quit, and singularly enough, he died in the very last week of his tenancy.'

The Rector of East Mersea

The impact of Sabine's anger may well have hastened his end, for Sabine in a rage was capable of alarming people far more robust. The biting phrase 'a poor, blanched creature, like sea-kale but not so tall', written forty years after, when the fires of his passionate nature were burning low, makes one wonder just what he actually said at the time.

In the following year, 1877, Sabine was again in Devon for quite another reason. The church at Staverton, near Totnes, at that time contained a number of memorials to the Gould family. He received from the vicar 'an appalling letter' which informed him that the architect of the Dean and Chapter, one Ewan Christian, had undertaken the 'restoration' of Staverton church. It described how the ledger-stones and Gould memorials had been torn up and thrown into the graveyard and the family vault filled with concrete. The only hope of saving anything, the vicar warned him, was to go down at once. To one with Sabine's exaggerated veneration for the past there could only be one possible answer. He dashed down to Devon and was only just in time, for on arrival he found that the only way to preserve the discarded ledger-stones from complete destruction was to remove them at his own expense to Lew Trenchard.

It is a curious and significant fact that this action has been held against him ever since. Why it is hard to imagine, for he had no power to replace the stones in Staverton church, and unless he had removed them no trace of them would now remain. They are now fastened to the walls of Lew Trenchard church and are often commented upon adversely by visitors. It is perhaps in keeping with our present day muddle-headed respect for officialdom that no one pauses to criticise the high-handed vandalism of the Dean and Chapter, who would cheerfully have destroyed the Gould memorials without even consulting the vicar of the parish or the living descendants of those commemorated. 'What vicar and Diocesan Advisory Committee would allow a squarson to remove tablets from other churches and put them

The Rector of East Mersea

up in his own as Baring-Gould did?' asks John Betjeman in the introduction to Purcell's *Onward, Christian Soldier*. Yet it was upon the advice of the vicar of Staverton that Sabine acted, in an attempt to reduce the wanton damage. All his life Sabine was constantly at war with those—and they were many—who in any way undervalued the heritage of the past. His instinct was always to preserve and not to destroy. The Staverton memorials were not an isolated instance due solely to an inflated family pride, but an example of the trouble he took to save for posterity anything of historical or antiquarian interest that would otherwise have been lost, whether it was a menhir, a folk-song, an ornate ceiling, or a tombstone. In his time much that was old, interesting and beautiful was being forgotten, torn down, or thrown upon the scrap-heap, and he fought fiercely, sometimes savagely, to save them. Who today dares blame him? Later chapters of this book will deal with this fight more fully, for it played a great part in his life. It cannot be denied that at times his enthusiasm and impetuosity led him into using methods not altogether above criticism, but in the case of the Staverton memorials that criticism has surely been misplaced.

It was while he was in Devon over the Staverton affair that Sabine began the restoration of Lew Trenchard church. At his own expense, the deal pews installed by his grandfather were removed and the ancient oak ones, which he had saved as a boy, were replaced, together with a number of excellent copies, which have weathered so well that it is now hard to tell which are the originals.

But there is certainly another side to the picture. As far as one can make out, East Mersea did not see much of its rector that year. Just as in 1847 Sabine's ill-health had given his father an excellent excuse for leaving England and returning to his beloved Europe, so thirty years later the health of his second daughter Margaret, and a return of his own chest trouble, provided Sabine with reason to leave the damp, marshy island of Mersea, with its

The Rector of East Mersea

bitter east winds, to the care of the long-suffering Gatrill, while he transferred his whole family to Freiburg im Breisgau.

For his eldest daughter Mary, at least, Freiburg provided a lifelong memory. She was now eight years old and to her awakening mind it was a dream of exquisite loveliness. She was always deeply sensitive to beauty and after the drab mud-flats of Essex, the glory of the autumn woods was sheer joy. The tracery of the cathedral, too, impressed her deeply, young as she was, and to the end of her days she loved to recall one unforgettable service to which she was taken by her parents, when the only light was provided by the hundreds of candles carried by the worshippers. At Freiburg, too, she had her first introduction to grand opera, which was to remain for her a lifelong passion. So small were Mary and Margaret that they were allowed to share one seat between them. But how they loved it!

From Freiburg Sabine sent an impulsive order to Sutton, the nurseryman, for 600 bird-cherries to be planted in Lew Wood. They never really succeeded in the moist, mild climate there, where there are few autumn frosts to turn the colour of the leaves before they fall, but the rhododendron bushes he planted all along the Tavistock road remain as a memorial to his love of colour in life.

It must have been about this time, too, that Sabine took his whole family on a walking tour through the Black Forest, though it is impossible to fix the exact date. He makes no mention of it in his *Reminiscences*, but Mary often spoke of it. Picture the tall figure of Sabine, dressed as ever in clerical black, striding ahead, leading with one hand a horse harnessed to a farm cart and in the other hand holding a book from which he read as he walked. Grace, his wife, followed with the children, Mary, Margaret and Edward trotting behind or riding on the cart when they grew tired. The tail of the procession was brought up by a sturdy German girl pushing a perambulator, quite a new invention in those days. In this slept Veronica, the latest addition to the family. They would pass the night in some little hamlet, nestling amid the great woods, at times sleeping at tiny inns that seemed to Mary to come straight out of Grimm's *Fairy Tales*. At other times they were the guests of kindly parish priests with whom Sabine spent long hours in learned theological debate. Every Sunday they stayed where they were and attended the village church. On one occasion a particularly charming old priest, with whom they had lodged the previous night, suddenly realised that he had Sabine in a position in which he could not possibly answer back. Tossing aside his notes and beaming from ear to ear he preached an extemporary sermon on heresy in general and the Church of England in particular, and then, immediately after the service, invited them all to share his midday meal.

How long their holiday lasted or where their meanderings led them has long been forgotten. Only down the years comes the gentle memory of Mary's voice, telling of sunlit summer days as they wandered through an enchanted Hansel and Gretel wonderland of forest and flowers and woodcutters. Once at least reality caught up with them, for a village they entered was stricken with typhoid fever. Mary was thirsty after the day's walk, to give her water or milk seemed too risky and she had her first drink of German beer. Years after she recalled how she climbed on a chair to see the time by a great grandfather clock and was deeply puzzled by the fact that not only the hands but the whole face seemed to be going round and round.

The climate of Freiburg suited little Margaret so well that a few years later she and Mary were sent there to be educated at a convent school. Sabine stipulated that no attempt should be made to persuade the girls to become Roman Catholics and the German nuns kept the agreement faithfully. The tiny flower-like Margaret was the pet of the whole school and her health improved greatly, but Mary was never really well or entirely happy there. In later days she would recall her schooldays with mixed feelings. Germany for her meant the beauty of the Black

Page 71: *The Wye Cottages, typical examples of the cottages built by Sabine Baring-Gould on the Lew Trenchard estate. He designed them himself, for he would never employ an architect, and they were constructed of local material by local craftsmen.*

Dunsland, the home of Sabine's son-in-law, A. W. H. Dickinson. Much of the panelling at Lew House was copied from that here. Dunsland became the property of the National Trust, but was destroyed by fire on the night of 17 November 1967.

Page 72: *'The vagaries of clerical dress'. Commissioned in 1920 and drawn by Sabine's eldest grandson, Arscott Dickinson, this illustration is all that can now be traced of the third volume of Sabine's* Reminiscences. *The manuscript on which he was working at the time of his death seems to have been lost, destroyed or possibly suppressed.*

The Rector of East Mersea

Forest; the patient kindness of the nuns; and the revolting taste of the sauerkraut she was forced to eat. Teaching methods in the Germany of those days were severe and discipline was strict. The girls were taught to play the piano by a music master who stood in the middle of a small music room, armed with a cane. The pupils sat at pianos ranged round the wall and played the same piece simultaneously. Woe betide the one who struck a wrong note or played out of time with the rest!

While at East Mersea Sabine added yet another member to his household: he persuaded the village schoolteacher, Miss Biggs, to come and live with them and act as governess to the children. She was a woman of high character and a fierce integrity, to whose training Mary always paid high tribute, but in later life she became so very strict that Sabine's younger daughters were frankly terrified of her. She remained with the Baring-Goulds long after all the children had grown up, and finally died in Lew Trenchard.

Of Sabine's pastoral work in East Mersea we know very little. That it was not particularly successful is obvious from his references to it, for he returned to the subject more than once in his *Reminiscences*. He had succeeded at Horbury and was to do so again in a different way when he finally returned to Devon. His slighting references to East Mersea may have been a form of self-justification for his failure there. Yet it was during his sojourn in East Mersea that his powers as a preacher developed. Those were the days of hour-long, dreary sermons, but in preaching as in all else he was something of a rebel. He seldom preached for more than ten minutes, or at most a quarter of an hour, taking one point only and hammering it home with all the force of his nature. This, like all innovations, proved unpopular in some quarters. On one occasion his farmer parishioners dared to protest, claiming bitterly that his sermons were so short that the congregation was never given time to get comfortably to sleep before being called upon to stand for the concluding hymn.

The Rector of East Mersea

There were those who did appreciate his sermons, however, and five books of them were published during the time he was rector of East Mersea. They show that his preaching was simple, forceful, and at times even abrupt. He never minced matters. He had in fact the greatest merit that any public speaker can possess: having made his point he knew when to stop.

Despite his obvious dislike both of the place and the people Sabine remained at East Mersea until, in 1881, his uncle Charles Baring-Gould, who had been rector of Lew Trenchard for over forty-eight years, died as quietly and unobtrusively as he had lived. He had spent the whole of his adult life in the little Devonshire parish and by Sabine's account he was a gentle, kindly and well-intentioned man, but in no way brilliant or outstanding. He was by inclination a High Churchman but was far too retiring to take any active part in the religious controversies of his day.

Charles Baring-Gould died on 15 February 1881, and in June of the same year, Sabine presented himself to the family living and was instituted by the Bishop of Exeter on 19 July. It was to be his last move.

6

Home at Last

Few men have been able to start a new life of their own choice at the age of forty-seven and even fewer have had the chance to carry it on under almost ideal conditions for another forty-three years, as Sabine did. He was, as we have seen, instituted in 1881 and when he died in 1924 he was still rector of Lew Trenchard. His position there was unusual, for he was a 'squarson', both squire and parson of the parish. Even in his day this was rare, for the eldest son of a landowning family rarely took Holy Orders.

For centuries village life centred round two pivots, the manor and the rectory. The manor was expected to give employment in one way or another to the whole parish. The squire often farmed the home farm himself and had a practical knowledge of his tenants' difficulties in a bad year. He not only employed farm-workers, gardeners, stablehands and gamekeepers, but an estate mason, a quarryman, a hedger, a carpenter and a blacksmith as well. The village girls found work in the manor house and were trained by the squire's wife. The young men of the village knew that if they married a girl who had worked in the manor kitchen, they had a good chance of having a wife who could really cook,

Home at Last

and the girls knew in consequence that to have worked there improved their chances of matrimony. There was an enormous difference between the lot of a member of the servants' hall in a country house and that of the pathetic maid-of-all-work in some small town lodging-house.

The system was of course open to many abuses. It placed far too much power in the hands of one man. An extravagant, selfish, absentee landlord, who left the care of his estate to an agent, who cared for nothing but collecting the rent and doing a minimum of repairs in return, could bring misery to the whole village, as could the game-mad sporting squire concerned more for the welfare of his pheasants than his tenants. On the other hand, a resident squire with a strong sense of his responsibilities, married to a capable and kindly wife, could provide a benevolent autocracy not to be despised.

The rectory was in a somewhat similar, if less powerful, position. There may have been few country parsons in the nineteenth century who were willing or able to live up to the ideal set by George Herbert 200 years previously, but he had at least provided a standard which could act as guide to many generations of parish priests. The sick, aged and destitute did turn instinctively to the rectory for help and it was almost always to some extent forthcoming. During the nineteenth century a third pivot, the village school, was added. Today all three have of course received their death-blow.

Soon after his return to Lew Trenchard, Sabine was made a magistrate and, as well as being squire and rector, he became ex-officio chairman of the 'Church' school. Once a schoolmaster, always a schoolmaster: for many years he visited the school regularly and himself gave the children their scripture lessons, which, from the accounts of elderly people who learned from him, continued to retain much of the originality and interest that had helped to make his Mission at Horbury Brig successful. He also took pains to encourage and improve the general standard

Home at Last

of education, especially in English composition and verse writing, for which he gave prizes and which he often judged himself. On 22 November 1923, only six weeks before his death, he wrote to Mr F. C. Doidge, then headmaster of Lew Trenchard school:

'Dear Mr Doidge,
   Thank you greatly for sending me the two copies of verses exhibiting considerable graceful taste and fancy. The lesson to be impressed on the versifier is that poetry really consists of the disclosure of an idea.
   The lines of Spry should link to the expression of the thought that in Nature is promise and no despondency. The fall of the fading leaf gives . . . of the swelling of the Spring Bud—that in death is Life's renewal.
   Avery's lines disclose graceful poetry. As far as I can see they should lead up to the conception that life does not consist only of that which is physical and mental but has its completion and . . . in the recognition of the third element, the spiritual.
   I am sorry not to have acknowledged the . . . but I have been ill in bed, ever since Sunday.
                                I remain
                                   yrs truly
                                      S. Baring-Gould

The paper on which the letter is written is now much discoloured and the ink faded; Sabine was near his end and his minute handwriting had become unusually hard to read. But the clarity of his mind emerges, and the interest that he continued to take in the children of his parishioners.

It seems strange today that Sabine was for many years permitted to employ an assistant curate to help with the pastoral work of a single small parish of under 200 inhabitants. For a lazy man this would have led to complete stagnation, but to one of his restlessly energetic nature, it allowed a freedom to pursue his many activities in a way few people have ever been lucky enough to do at any period of history. Among the assistant clergy who worked under him, two might be selected for mention. The

Home at Last

first was his own half-brother Arthur, who later became chaplain to Dartmoor Prison, then curate at Brixham and finally vicar of St Martin's, Haverfordwest. Though overshadowed by Sabine, Arthur was a remarkable man, who like Sabine lived to a great age and continued to work to the end, and like Sabine had his own ways of doing things. The Baring-Gould clergy were a long-lived breed: Charles was rector of Lew Trenchard for forty-nine years, Sabine for forty-three, and Arthur was vicar of Haverfordwest for forty-seven.

The following account of Arthur Baring-Gould is taken from a paper *Great Welsh Churchmen and their Prayers* and is quoted here because it gives us a glimpse of a personality as unusual as Sabine's:

> 'What a wonderful old Saint, that is. Surely he can't be long for this world. He's almost in the other already.' So said one who heard Arthur Baring-Gould preach, not long before he died, still in harness as Vicar of St Martin's, Haverfordwest. That quality of personal holiness, unmistakable whether he was at the altar, in the pulpit, or pottering in the greenhouse in a battered panama hat and green baize apron, had not come easily with the years. It resulted from hard toil, constant prayer, recurring domestic tragedy and suffering and, in the last years increasing blindness. And he carried it with the humility and humour which gave it the hallmark of genuineness.
>
> ... But he could be a stern pastor, too, as on the occasion of his briefest sermon. 'Last Sunday I rebuked you for your unfaithfulness at 8. I observed no improvement today. I am fed up with you. And now to God the Father. . . .'

The last time he left Wales was to visit his old friend Harvey Dickinson, when both of them were nearly ninety years old.

Arthur's mother, the second Mrs Edward Baring-Gould, continued to live in Lew Trenchard parish for many years at a house called Ardoch Lodge. Here Mary, who was the same age as Arthur's sister Lilah, saw a great deal of this devout old lady, who had strict views on Sabbath observance. Every Saturday

Home at Last

night she removed all the children's books except the Bible and the *Pilgrim's Progress*, and the only game that she permitted on Sunday was one in which texts from the Bible were built up by arranging letters drawn in turn from a common pool.

Sabine's last curate, the Rev Gilbert Arundell, was a very different type of man. During Sabine's old age he did the greater part of the work of the parish and succeeded him as rector in 1924. He was an excellent if late example of that curious and almost extinct phenomenon, the sporting parson. These men were common in Devon as elsewhere during the nineteenth century. Drawn from the ranks of the younger sons of the squirearchy, they shared with the majority of their parishioners a passion for field sports. They varied from men who retained a high sense of their duty as parish priests to out-and-out rogues of the type depicted by Blackmore in *The Maid of Sker*. Sabine was personally familiar with both varieties. In the chapter 'Hunting Parsons' in his book *Old Country Life* he wrote:

> I was one day on top of a coach along with two farmers, one from the parish of Jack Russell, another from that of another hunting parson, whom we will call Jack Hannaford. They were discussing their relative parsons. Then he who was under Hannaford told a scurvy tale of him, whereat his companion said: 'Tell 'ee what, all the world knows what your pa'sson be; but as for old Jack Russell, up and down his backbone, he's as good a Christian, as worthy a pastor, and as true a gentleman as I ever seed.'

Gilbert Arundell did not apparently ride to hounds, though he followed on foot, but he always looked more at home wearing cricket flannels in summer, or carrying a shotgun in winter, than he did when wearing a cassock. He was outstanding at cricket; a good forcing bat and an unusually fine wicket-keeper. This in one way gave him the advantage over Sabine, for a rural community takes readily to a man who enjoys sharing its recreations.

Home at Last

For many years, too, there lived in the parish a couple who supported Sabine loyally and on whose help he could always depend, a Mr and Mrs Sperling of Coombe Trenchard. Sabine obtained permission to sell off the old and dilapidated rectory and build a new one for his successors nearer to the church, while he himself continued to live at Lew House. The Sperlings purchased the former rectory and in course of years completely transformed it, making of it a beautiful mansion that they renamed Coombe Trenchard. Here they lived in a style that was, in Devon at least, already fast disappearing. Mr Sperling kept his own pack of hounds and paid the hunt servants out of his own pocket, being in consequence invariably known as 'the Maister'. He also rented the sporting rights of the Lew Trenchard estate from Sabine, kept a gamekeeper and raised pheasants on a large scale. Mrs Sperling had a passion for gardening and the money to indulge it, employing four gardeners, working indefatigably herself and coercing her numerous guests into assisting her on all possible occasions. There was a large indoor staff as well.

The Sperlings invariably attended church on Sunday mornings and insisted on their staff doing so in the evenings. Sabine himself had his large and strictly disciplined family—and also his staff and his tenants, many of whom went to church from reasons of expediency, though not from compulsion, for Sabine was a dictator only where his own family was concerned; add to these his step-mother and her household from Ardoch Lodge, the headmaster of the church school on Lewdown, the tenants of the Dower House, and his curate's wife and family, and Sabine had a ready-made congregation that filled his church each week.

In fact in those days Sundays held no counter-attractions, and Sabine also drew people to his church from neighbouring parishes by his forceful preaching. In consequence he never, during the greater part of his time at Lew Trenchard, suffered the wretched experience that has dogged so many country clergy of preaching week after week to an almost empty church.

Home at Last

In this congenial atmosphere he mellowed and throve exceedingly. At Lew Trenchard his boundless energy and enthusiasm were at last fully occupied in that multiplicity of congenial tasks which for him spelt happiness. Continuous mental and physical activity were equally necessary to his well-being and he once wrote: 'It is change of work, rather than cessation from work that refreshes the mental powers.' He might well have taken as his motto the old Westcountry adage 'Do zummat. Do good if 'ee can, but do zummat'.

Ecclesiastical and local history, the study of the antiquities with which Dartmoor and the Cornish moors abounded, architecture, folklore and the byways of medieval literature, fascinated him and he wrote of them all, besides completing at least one novel yearly. At the same time he threw himself into the task of collecting the almost-forgotten local folk-songs, and set about the restoration of his little church and the rebuilding of his home, his farms and all the cottages on his estate.

For some reason he hated architects and himself designed all the houses that he built, sometimes with curious results. The new rectory was a case in point. Constructed of stone and slate quarried on the estate, it is like everything he touched, both original and beautiful, but the second flight of stairs was an afterthought and is more nearly vertical than stairs have any business to be. It is said that the construction of two of the cottages that he designed was well advanced before anyone noticed that he had forgotten the front doors, but they are well built, comfortable to live in, and pleasing to the eye. Standing in a position that catches all the sun, is sheltered from the prevailing westerly winds and commands a superb view, they are still occupied.

His curiosity and capacity for work seemed to increase rather than diminish with the years. He wrote about everything that interested him, seldom troubling to verify a fact or look up a reference, depending utterly on his memory. He was a natural populariser and a born story-teller; one who could write on

Home at Last

subjects ranging from candle-snuffers to werewolves as though they were the one thing in life that really interested him. He spent many hours daily at his desk in the library, but he never resembled that type of scholarly parson who, having acquired a remote rural living, spends his whole life surrounded by his books, 'invisible to his flock all the week and incomprehensible to them on Sundays', for when not actually writing he was always on the move.

In the course of years a number of legends have grown up about Sabine and his ways; so many indeed that it is at times very hard to sift fact from fiction. They stem from two sources. In the first place there are the stories told of him by his contemporaries and not always entirely accurately remembered by their children. These are for the most part reliable in all but minor details. To give one example: an old woman in the parish had a sick pig and asked Sabine to pray for its recovery. He visited the sty, pointed his stick at the pig and said with great solemnity: 'Pig! If thou livest, thou livest and if thou diest thou diest'. The pig recovered and the matter seemed forgotten until Sabine himself fell ill with a quinsy, whereupon the old woman presented herself at Lew House and demanded to see him. Pointing her stick at him, she declaimed: 'Parson! If thou livest thou livest and if thou diest thou diest'. Sabine at this burst into such a fit of laughter that the quinsy broke and like the pig he recovered. Four different people have told this story to the writer. Their versions have been substantially the same, but they have all differed as to the cottage in which the old woman lived.

The second type of story told about Sabine is less kindly and far less reliable. Lew House has for many years been let as an hotel, though it still belongs to the Baring-Goulds. While dining there one evening, one of Sabine's grandsons overheard a guest saying: 'He was a horrible old man. He even made his daughters paint all the ceilings'. Several of the younger daughters in question were still alive at that time and the grandson made careful enquiries, being interested, if not particularly horrified. The story proved to be a complete fabrication, though Margaret (Daisy), who was a trained artist, did paint a series of panels depicting the virtues, which are still to be seen in the very room in which the story was told. Several similar but much more damaging stories still go the rounds, put about in ignorance or with deliberate malice by visitors who never knew him.

Another widely circulated story is that he always visited his parishioners in state, riding in a carriage drawn by two horses and driven by a liveried coachman. Like much else that is told of him this is not only untrue, but gives an entirely false impression of his character, for he was a man who disliked ostentation in any form. In reality, for a number of years he did his visiting on foot, covering many miles daily with his long, swinging stride. He had however the disconcerting habit of doing all his regular visiting in the morning, entering and leaving each house somewhat abruptly and seldom staying for more than a few minutes, for as he well knew he had not the gift for cheerful, easy small-talk. But on leaving he usually left behind him some small gift of sweets for the children or bulbs for the garden. As years went by he took to driving around, perched on the high seat of a dog-cart, driven by a redoubtable character, Charlie Dustan, his groom and general factotum.

There were in fact few men for whom the trappings of wealth and position had less interest. As rector and squire of Lew Trenchard he was still as careless of outward appearances as on that day, many years before, when he arrived at Horbury to begin his curacy, carrying the 'black slug' draped across his shoulders. Charlie Dustan was not the stately coachman of tradition, though he did sport a top hat when driving Sabine round the parish. He looked after the horses, weeded the garden paths and taught generations of Sabine's descendants the first stages of horsemanship. Mary Dickinson's sons were among those he

Home at Last

taught to ride on an aged Dartmoor pony called Winnie, which had often carried Mary before her marriage and had somehow acquired the Baring-Gould gift of longevity. In an emergency Charlie would spruce himself up and wait at table, bringing to the dining-room a strong atmosphere of the stable.

The Baring-Goulds did possess a family carriage which was seldom used unless a number of them were invited to a party or a dance. Charlie would then act as coachman, but being a convivial soul, the long wait and good refreshments sometimes proved too much for him, so there were times when Sabine or one of his daughters had perforce to take the reins on the return journey and Charlie would arrive back sleeping peacefully inside the carriage. No one really minded very much for Charlie was a privileged person, a family retainer of an almost-forgotten type who completely identified himself with his employer. 'Us 'ave a new baby a-comin' again,' he said confidentially to a visitor whom he was fetching from Coryton station, 'so us'll 'ave to sell another book again quick.'

Year after year the new babies continued to arrive with unfailing regularity, but no one heard Grace complain. The nearest she came to doing so was on the occasion of Mary's wedding, when she said to one of her younger daughters: 'Of course I love you all, my dears, but I do hope Mary will not produce quite so many children to love as I have done.' Without his capacity for writing and selling his books quickly, Sabine would often have found himself in serious financial difficulties, which is no doubt one of the reasons why his work sometimes shows signs of being over-hurried. Writing was never an art to be practised for art's sake: he wrote easily and fluently, but novel-writing especially often irked him, though he admitted that once a story had got under way, the characters were apt to take charge to such an extent that he was quite sorry to be done with them. But he wrote largely for the money that his books brought in, of which he was always in need. Whatever his income, he always

Home at Last

lived up to it and sometimes above it. His ever-growing family had to be fed, clothed and educated, and his impulsive nature led him into sudden bursts of expenditure on anything that seemed to him beautiful, interesting or curious. The 600 bird-cherry trees, already mentioned, ordered on the spur of the moment for planting in Lew Wood, were only one small example. He was an inveterate book-buyer, and the type of book that interested him was often expensive; nor could he ever resist purchasing pictures, antique furniture, or curios that took his fancy. On one occasion, while still at East Mersea, he bought a fine walnut cabinet at a sale; he was at the time hard-pressed for money and excused his extravagance to himself by presenting it to his daughter Mary on her sixth birthday. The cabinet came to Lew Trenchard when they moved, and was put in a place of honour, where it remained until, somewhat to his chagrin, Mary remembered that it was hers and removed it to her new home at Dunsland after her marriage.

On railway fares alone he must have spent a small fortune, for he never neglected any excuse for travel. He frankly loved the good things of life and enjoyed fine food, especially game. Many of his letters to Mary, written after her marriage, contain thanks for pheasants and woodcock sent him from Dunsland by her husband. All his life he was a large and rapid eater, but the food that he consumed seemed to be burnt up by the fires of nervous energy within him and his long, wiry frame never put on weight or acquired a middle-age spread.

It was not, however, upon luxuries that the bulk of his income was spent. While still a boy he had resolved that one day he would attempt three things. The first was to reform the spiritual and moral life of Lew Trenchard parish; the second was to restore the church; and the third was to improve and make comfortable all the farms, cottages and houses on the estate, including Lew House. Now thirty years later his energy still unimpaired, he was at last in the position to carry them out. To

Home at Last

these ends he worked ceaselessly for over forty years; having no sympathy with idleness in any form he spared neither himself nor his family.

Mary would often describe a typical Sunday in her girlhood. She rose and attended Holy Communion at 8 am. At 10 she taught in the Sunday School. At 11 she played the organ at Matins. Her afternoon was spent again teaching in the Sunday School, her pupils including numerous small brothers and sisters. At Evensong she once more acted as organist. When supper was over there were family prayers for the older members of the family; after which, greatly daring, she would go to the piano and sing the refrain of one of her father's church songs, but not in the spirit in which he had intended it, when he wrote the words:

> Sunday is over, Sunday is past,
> The Day of Rejoicing is closing AT LAST.

One would expect to hear that Mary after her marriage never again went voluntarily to church, but in reality the reverse was the case and the habit of unfailing church attendance, formed in youth, remained with her throughout her life.

Where his daughters were concerned Sabine was a complete autocrat. He even insisted on designing Mary's frock for her first county ball, and in consequence she went in an agony of self-consciousness, clad in flowing classical draperies, in startling contrast to the fussy Victorian ball-dresses of the other girls. It was not until many years later that she learned that, to the fury of the girls, the men had talked of nothing all the evening but the beautiful Miss Baring-Gould and her wonderful dress. In later years her younger sisters staged a minor revolt. They even dared to smoke, though they always did so up one of the great open chimneys, so that the rising wood-smoke would carry away the scent of tobacco. On one occasion when, as a married woman

Home at Last

with growing children of her own, Mary was staying at Lew House, one of her younger sisters was in the room with her, smoking a cigarette. The old man entered suddenly, and without hesitation Mary took the cigarette from the girl's fingers and smoked, for the only time in her life. For once in his life Sabine was too startled to speak. He himself never smoked until at seventy he was ordered medicated tobacco for his throat. The habit once formed, he smoked a pipe for the last twenty years of his life.

If in his dealings with his daughters he was autocratic, towards his sons Sabine was by modern standards unduly severe. At school they received little or no pocket money and though they were all intelligent not one of them went on from school to the University. As soon as their schooling was over the old eagle drove his male fledgelings from the nest to fend for themselves.

Perhaps because of his own upbringing, perhaps because of his advanced political views, Sabine had little use for that English upper-middle class institution, the great public school, or for that matter for schools of any kind. The girls for the most part received little more education than that which Miss Biggs could provide, and the boys were sent to local grammar schools. Henry alone had a real public-school education and his fees at Winchester were paid by a wealthy relative. 'The dark-eyed formidable boys', as Cecil Sharp, the collector of folk-songs, once called them, scattered far.

From the point of view of the estate for which he himself worked so hard, Sabine made the mistake of sending his eldest son, Edward, to the United States while still a youth. He did not return until, a married man, he came to London to found his own successful business in the City, only leaving it to serve in the first World War. He was a man of great kindness and integrity, with a gift for financial matters—a throwback to the banker Barings of the eighteenth century; but he was by necessity and inclination a town dweller, never really at home in the country,

Home at Last

and always content to leave the care of the estate to an agent. His three children all settled in the United States, and after the death of his first wife the Baring-Goulds, though still owning the property, have remained absentee landlords.

Sabine's second son, Julian, was sent straight from school to work in an arsenic mine near Tavistock, and from there he went to serve under that extraordinarily picturesque Devonian, Rajah Brooke, who had made himself ruler of Sarawak. Julian married and had three sons and a daughter. The eldest son died in infancy and both the other two were killed in action during the second World War, as was their cousin Gervaise Tinley, DFC, the only son of Colonel Frank Newport Tinley and Cicely, Sabine's eighth daughter.

William Baring-Gould, Sabine's third son, also went to the United States, leaving England with a hundred pounds in his pocket and orders to make his own way in the world. His elder brother, Edward, gave him an introduction to a friend in Minneapolis, a Mr E. G. Walton, with whom he was associated in business for some years. Later, though by this time he had become an American citizen, he was made British consul in Minneapolis and did much to promote good Anglo-American relations there. He died in 1920, leaving one son, William Stuart Baring-Gould, who worked on the staff of the American periodical *Time* and wrote among other things an amusing 'biography' of Sherlock Holmes.

Henry, Sabine's next son, was sent straight from Winchester to work in the Bristol Docks, at that time reputed to be one of the roughest places in England. From there he followed Edward and William to America, returning almost penniless some five years later to be packed off almost immediately to a plantation in Malaya, where he died of fever.

Sabine fully realised what hardships his severity could and did impose on his sons, but he was determined to make them capable of standing on their own feet from an early age and in this his

Home at Last

political outlook undoubtedly influenced him. On 30 November 1903, when Henry was only eighteen years old, he wrote to Mary:

> I saw Harry who has been through hard times. He has to sit in the kitchen and has no room to himself. Even his bedroom is not his own for the man and his boy also sleep in it. . . . He has borne it gallantly and without complaint—devoured by fleas, and it has done him good. He has learnt to know and be on a footing with the British working man and that is an asset for life.

John, Sabine's youngest son, also went to Malaya. He returned to serve at first in the North Devon Yeomanry in the same squadron as his nephew, Arscott Dickinson, who was only three years younger than himself. Later he transferred into the Royal Flying Corps and was severely wounded. After the war he returned to the Far East; served again in the Royal Air Force in the second World War and finally settled in Rhodesia.

Of the fourteen children who grew to maturity, all the daughters and all the sons, except Henry, married and had families. In all Sabine and Grace had twenty-nine grandchildren, most of whom in their turn had families. It is a curious and perhaps significant fact that not one has entered the Church, with the exception of the present writer, who was not ordained until he was sixty, while none of Sabine's daughters and only one of his grand-daughters married a clergyman.

To those who depended on him for their livelihood, Sabine behaved with consistent kindness and consideration. It is typical of his complicated nature that he could combine without any sense of incongruity what was in some ways an almost feudal outlook towards his tenants and parishioners with his advanced political views. This may be hard to understand, but in it lies the key to many of his actions. He employed, for example, a considerable number of men on the estate in one way or another. Rather than catch any one of these idling as he drove around the

Home at Last

parish, he had bells fastened to the harness of his horse so as to give timely warning of his approach.

His love for his parishioners was genuine and he was extraordinarily tolerant of their foibles; a fact that is particularly worthy of note when one compares it with his impatience and intolerance in other directions, especially in his dealings with his ecclesiastical superiors, with whom he was constantly at war. Where they were concerned he knew only too well how unpopular he was. He once wrote: 'I think that it is not improbable that both the Archbishop of York and Claughton of Rochester had inserted my name in the Episcopal "Black Book", for I had shown precious little deference to either.'

We all have in youth certain vague hopes and ambitions, but in Sabine they were clearly defined and he never deviated from them. Despite his peculiarities, there was in him a certain unique quality, even a touch of greatness, which was recognised, sometimes rather grudgingly, by all with whom he came in personal contact, but which was almost invariably misunderstood.

It is true that he was greatly favoured by fortune. Probably at no other period of history and in no other circumstances could he have lived so untrammelled a life or have had the chance to achieve all that he did. But it was his own energy and the certainty in his own mind that he was called upon to do these things that overcame all obstacles and made it possible for him to live to see many of his youthful dreams turn to realities.

7

The Rector of Lew Trenchard

The first of the three tasks that Sabine set himself to perform when he came to Lew Trenchard, 'the spiritual rousing of the people', as he called it, certainly offered him a challenge, for religious life in the parish had for long been moribund.

In 1862, two years before his ordination, while he was still working as a schoolmaster at Hurstpierpoint, Sabine had spent Christmas at Lew House and had written in his diary:

> Christmas Day. Alone except for my brother in Lew House. The rats were celebrating Noël . . . they kept me awake.
> Presently I heard the distant strains of carol singers and the groaning accompanyment of a bass-viol. I ascertained in the morning that the performers were the choir of the Meeting House. The Church, buried in sleep, did not sing to greet the Saviour's birth. The Chapel choir itinerated all night . . . and at their return were all the worse for liquor,
> In Church this morning there were only twelve persons, of these nearly all were from the Rectory.

Twenty years later, after his induction, at the first Easter Communion that he celebrated, it was even worse, for there were

The Rector of Lew Trenchard

only nine communicants all told, 'mainly officials'. In the old Parish Register he wrote: 'Behold your house is left unto you desolate, until ye shall say, Blessed is He that cometh in the Name of the Lord.' This situation has some interest to a country clergyman of today, who has to combat each Sunday the rival attractions of motor-cycle 'scrambles', trips to the seaside and the ever-present inducement to sit comfortably at home and watch television, for he is inclined to imagine that before these distractions existed the rural population came regularly to church. There may have been places and periods when this was so, but the records show conclusively that Lew Trenchard, a century ago, was not one of them. In White's *History, Gazetteer, and Directory of Devonshire, 1850*, the population of the parish is given as 527. Today it has fallen to less than a third of that number, but in 1962 there were thirty-one Christmas communicants as against the twelve mentioned by Sabine in 1862, and thirty-five Easter communicants compared with the nine he refers to in 1882. When Sabine returned to Lew Trenchard he had no illusions about the difficulty and frustration facing anyone trying to awaken spiritual feeling in a place where it has become run down; both at Dalton and at East Mersea he had personal experience of it.

> On entering Holy Orders there is one consideration that is often overlooked—the prospect of a life, and best efforts, being, as far as man can see, wholly thrown away.
>
> Many an earnest and devout clergyman is planted in some unsuitable living, among intractable people, without token of his labour producing any effect. A thousand hearts are broken, a thousand such lives wasted, long cherished and fervent hopes killed.... To work day after day, year after year, without recognition or appreciation takes all the heart out of him. It should not be so, but so it is.

Sabine knew human nature pretty well—he could never have

The Rector of Lew Trenchard

been a successful novelist had he not done so. He was well aware that among many nominal Christians, religious conviction finds small place, and that the least personal affront is enough to make a lifelong churchgoer switch to some other place of worship, or even give up going anywhere at all. Probably every country clergyman could give instances from his own experience. Sabine certainly could and did. In his *Reminiscences* he quotes the retort of a village washerwoman to Mrs Baring-Gould, when exception was taken to the slovenly way in which the linen was returned: 'If you don't like my washing, I shall go to the Chapel and leave the Church'. He knew, too, the sadness of seeing good work ruined by home influences:

> Another trial the candidate will have to encounter is the neutralisation of his teaching among the children by home indifference and example. This applies to the young of the slums in a town, of the cottages in the country, to those of the mansions and of 'Society'. They are on a level. . . . As soon as the children come home, parental example undoes all the teaching in the Sunday School and the Church. Of course there are exceptions in all cases.

For the methods of the revivalist Sabine always felt a deep mistrust. For him the pulpit was the place where, week by week, year by year, he could make the sermon not an emotional substitute for worship, but a means of inculcating a life of regular prayer and devotion; for he saw the altar and not the pulpit as the focal point of Christian life. Everything else must be subordinate to the need to reawaken in his flock the true significance of the Holy Communion service, as the supreme act of worship. He was content to work slowly and patiently towards this end, but that it was to him of primary importance is clearly shown by a few lines that he wrote towards the end of his life:

> I think the happiest day of my life was the Easter of 1901, when I restored the Holy Eucharist to its proper place as the one service appointed by Christ for His Church.

The Rector of Lew Trenchard

His sermons were never used to display his own learning, and he never made the mistake of talking over the heads of his congregation or of talking down to them. In a letter to Mrs Joan Priestley, Arthur Baring Gould once described Sabine's sermons as being simple, homely, definite in doctrine and illustrated by interesting stories and personal experiences. They were invariably short and to the point, for Sabine was firmly convinced that anything worth saying could be said in ten minutes or at most a quarter of an hour. Though he could not help knowing his popularity as a preacher, he did not approve of it. The real reasons for churchgoing were for him summed up in the introduction to Morning and Evening Prayer in the Prayer Book, which stresses the need for repentance, worship, thanksgiving, intercession and the reading of Scripture, but makes no mention whatsoever of a sermon.

As a young man he had stayed in Wolverhampton with his puritanical uncle, the Rev Alexander Baring-Gould, and in his *Early Reminiscences* he describes the clash of ideas between them:

> I was talking one day with my uncle on Church service, when he said to me: 'I rather approve of Morning and Evening Prayers, as they sober and prepare the soul for the sermon.' 'Good Heavens!' I exclaimed, 'I do not view their relative positions in that light. We go to church to worship God. This is the substance. As for the sermon, it is the hors d'oeuvre, as at a dinner; like sardines on toast, we can do without it, or we can take it as an adjunct, but as nothing more.'

For anyone to come to church simply to hear a sermon, or to stay away merely because the preacher's style did not suit the listener's taste was to him repugnant. In consequence he went to considerable lengths not to let it be known whether he or his curate was going to preach. At times he even switched them round without warning, so his curate had always to be prepared to give an address at a moment's notice. That did not prevent

The Rector of Lew Trenchard

him from insisting that his curates conformed to his own time-limit of a quarter of an hour; if they exceeded it there would come an audible sigh from Sabine's stall, then a clearing of the throat and finally he would rise to his feet, whereupon his unfortunate assistant would hurriedly bring his discourse to a close.

Arthur Baring-Gould's daughter, Mrs Irene Widdicombe, had personal memories of Sabine's preaching. In a letter dated September 1965 she wrote:

> Uncle Sabine was very emotional. I have known him unable to finish a sermon because of something he said stirring him either to laughter or tears. . . .
> His sermons were a joy—so short, making but one point, that being quite enough for the Lew congregation—but he really made the point and it was not easy to forget. For my sister and myself it was a boon indeed, for as Grannie became too deaf to hear the sermon, she made us recount it to her as we went home [to Ardoch Lodge]. There was no brain fag at all when Uncle Sabine was the preacher, but it was a very different matter when it was Mr X. We were not in the habit of listening to him. By good chance one or other of us might have remembered the text and a sentence here and there, from which we had to improvise a sermon which would cover ourselves in Grannie's eyes. Very gratifying indeed it was when Grannie, at the end of our united efforts said: 'Dear X, he is certainly improving in his preaching.'

As we grow older we tend to remember only the exceptional and to believe that in our youth it was the normal, that all summers were hotter, and all winters colder than they are today; and we are probably completely wrong. Yet there is little else but the personal memories of ageing people on which an estimate of the rise and fall of church congregations can be based, for in the Church of England at any rate the only records kept are of the number of communicants, and at Lew Trenchard even these are missing. There was undoubtedly a great improvement in

The Rector of Lew Trenchard

church attendance during Sabine's ministry, as several of his letters to Mary clearly show. One of these is an undated, but interesting, Christmas letter, probably written about 1890, which is worth quoting *in extenso* as it gives us a glimpse, not only of his work as a parish priest, but of the widespread contacts and friendships that he retained throughout his life and of his attempts to preserve antiquities at any cost:

My Dearest Mary,
Many thanks to you and Harvey for having found out my weak point and pampering it. I shall enjoy the snipe and no mistake. We have a very merry, happy party here. Yesterday the church was lovely. Forty-four communicants and the church so crammed in the evening that many could not get in. All Coryton was there as well as Lew.

I had a curious collection of Christmas cards, one from an actress, one from two little children of a working woman in Edinburgh whom I have never seen, one from an innkeeper, one from a butler, one from a bagman and one from a potter. The actress was Alys Rees (Kate in Red Spider) [see chapter 11], the innkeeper was Whittaker in London and the butler Harry 'the Dook'. The bagman was a young socialist commercial I made great friends with in the Potteries and the potter is a hand in these latter.

Do you know who is the contractor for Poundstock church? I fear shocking havoc is being wrought there under the abused term 'restoration'. The old bench ends, if about to be turned out, I should like to secure. I think if you will have me I may run down for a night or two and see about them.

I remain
with best wishes for the New Year
yr affectionate father
S. Baring-Gould.

If the memories of surviving elderly people are to be trusted, it was not unusual to find every seat occupied in Lew Trenchard church, latecomers being obliged to stand, but probably this only happened occasionally, when parties of tourists and cycling clubs

The Rector of Lew Trenchard

timed their Sunday excursions to worship at Lew before starting on their return journey.

The fact that he was not a trained musician did not prevent Sabine from having strong views on church music. He was firmly convinced that in village churches it should all be strictly congregational; everyone should be encouraged to join in the responses and share in the singing. For this reason he placed the choir at the back of the church, where they could be heard but not seen, in the hope that their voices would lead on the congregation to take part instead of merely listening, as too often happens in Anglican churches. The results were at least hearty, though sometimes disconcerting to a sensitive ear. For years, only members of his family knew that Sabine kept two ear-plugs handy for insertion whenever one ardent but discordant member of his congregation was in church.

No service at which he officiated was dreary, for not only did his sermons catch and hold the attention of his hearers, but he took great pains always to bring out the full beauty of Cranmer's noble prose. The psalms were neither read nor badly rendered, as is so commonly the case in rural churches, but were sung antiphonally by himself and the congregation. To attend Lew Trenchard church when he was at the height of his powers was a revelation as to how the ancient liturgical services could be made to come to life. Yet he never succeeded in breaking down the old snobbish convention that has so often ruined the sense of brotherhood among Anglicans: the rigid if unwritten principle that the well-to-do attend Matins and their humbler brethren go to Evensong. At Leeson church, we read, the Rev George Alard had: 'a good collection of the neighbouring gentlefolk at Matins, a hearty assembly of the villagers at Evensong, a few "good" people at the early Celebration, and one or two old ladies for the Litany on Fridays.' Lew Trenchard only followed the usual pattern, which originally grew up, no doubt, in the days when those who went to Morning Prayer were certain of a

The Rector of Lew Trenchard

well-cooked Sunday dinner ready for them on their return. They could then doze over a book all the afternoon and eat a cold supper with a feeling of conscious rectitude because their domestic staff had been dragooned into attending Evensong at the parish church. The echo of this strange social division still lingers on in rural districts.

Sabine was a pioneer in a number of directions and it might fairly be claimed for him that he was among the first to do anything practical to help the cause of Christian reunion. Though a High Churchman and an indefatigable protagonist of the Catholic Revival in the Church of England, he was convinced that everyone in his parish was a member of his flock and their religious needs were his responsibility. There dwelt at that time a number of old people at the extreme end of the parish who could not be expected to walk as far as the parish church or the Methodist Chapel at Broadley. For them he held regular services in conjunction with the Methodist minister in a nearby farmhouse.

When first he took up the task of rousing what he described as the 'torpid religious feeling' in Lew Trenchard, he realised that a long-term policy was needed and that, as at Horbury Brig, he would have to begin with the children. For this reason the Scripture lessons in the village school and the work of the Sunday School were vitally important.

Curiously, among the many myths that have accumulated round Sabine's memory is one to the effect that he had little interest in children. William Purcell, in *Onward, Christian Soldier*, makes a point of this, saying that Sabine scarcely understood children at all, indeed barely noticed them; yet it is hard to imagine how this idea can be reconciled with the success of the Mission work at Horbury Brig, for children do not cling to a teacher's coat-tails or demand a story from him if he habitually ignores them. Despite Sabine's dictatorial attitude towards them, his huge family was devoted to him. Mary had many tales of

The Rector of Lew Trenchard

his understanding and sweetness to her as a little girl. Another daughter, Joan, who kept a detailed record of her father's sayings and doings, had a love and respect for him that amounted to veneration.

There are still in Lew Trenchard a few elderly people who retain memories of their Sunday School days and of his kindness towards them, for the Sunday School in his time had a remarkable vitality about it. The writer himself spent quite a lot of time at Lew House in his early childhood, and two personal memories may serve to illustrate Sabine's approach to his younger parishioners. The first is of a children's service in Lew Trenchard church, about the year 1905, when Sabine had already reached the age of seventy. Old people often find it hard to understand the very young and even those with the best intentions may lose touch with them, but Sabine's talk to the children that day has remained a vivid memory after more than sixty years. With the skill of a professional storyteller he fascinated his young audience as he described what life must have been like in Noah's Ark. They shuddered delightfully as he dramatised Noah's difficulties with the bad-tempered hippopotamus and laughed at his panic when the mouse was nearly trodden on by the elephant.

The other memory is of riding on an overcrowded farm wagon all the way to Dartmoor in company with the village children. The occasion was a Sunday School treat at which Sabine presided over a treasure hunt for pennies that he had previously hidden among the heather and boulders. (In 1963, the lady representing the parish at the Diocesan Conference had also as a child been on that wagon! She had equally clear and happy memories of Sabine's carefully prepared treasure hunt.)

The often-repeated story of his failing to recognise one of his own children at a party in his own house is true enough; the child was Joan, his seventh daughter. But tellers of the tale fail to realise that the inside of Lew House is dark even today, that it was much darker before electric light was installed, and that

The Rector of Lew Trenchard

Sabine's sight was very bad indeed. He had ruined it while reading by the light of a flickering ship's lantern during his return voyage from Iceland, and it had continued to deteriorate during many years of study, until he sometimes failed to recognise those to whom he spoke, whether children or adults. He read with his book only a few inches away from his face and in a half-light he was so blind that the village children would vie with one another for the honour of leading him home from Evensong on winter evenings. Mr Purcell dramatises the incident on the second page of *Onward, Christian Soldier*:

> He bent over her, stooping from his great height, a smile on his formidable falcon face: 'And whose little girl are you, my dear?'
> 'I'm yours, Daddy,' she sobbed.

Whether Joan really sobbed, I cannot say; but incidentally she certainly never called him 'Daddy', for all Sabine's children called him 'Papa'. The fact is that though he was undoubtedly severe towards his adolescent sons, autocratic when dealing with his daughters, and vitriolic when writing of those whose theology displeased him, all that was gentle in his nature rose to the surface in the presence of young children.

Before leaving the subject of his defective vision, an amusing story is told of him locally. Without his spectacles he was almost helpless, but he had the trick while preaching of pushing them up on to his forehead and immediately losing them. He would then produce another pair from the pocket of his cassock and use them until they, too, had been pushed up to join the first pair. On one occasion he was wearing two, some say three pairs, perched one above the other, and was vainly seeking them, without for one moment breaking the flow of his discourse. Anyone entering the church at that moment would have been greeted by the extraordinary sight of about half the congregation gesticulating and tapping their foreheads in a vain attempt to catch the preacher's eye to show him where the lost glasses had hidden themselves; an entirely wasted endeavour, as without them he was incapable of seeing what even those nearest to him were doing.

The mass of apparent contradictions in Sabine's character were as hard to understand during his lifetime as they are today. Mary, who was once told to open and read his correspondence while he was from home, remembered a letter from a lady who greatly admired his hymns, but hoped that he was no relation of the wicked novelist of the same name. Many of his novels do have touches of seeming heartlessness in descriptions of the very type of people for whom he worked unremittingly all his life. It was this that made J. M. Barrie, of gentle heart and completely different background, judging him entirely by his writings, attack him with unwonted fierceness in an article published in 1890 in the *Contemporary Review*.

Even in his firmly held religious convictions Sabine was at times strangely inconsistent. For the cause of the Catholic Revival in the Church of England he fought with the passion of a crusader. He would have died for the doctrine of Apostolic Succession, as the Tractarians understood it, but as already mentioned this in no way deterred him from disliking almost every bishop with whom he ever came in personal contact, and saying so on every possible occasion. Again, having given many years of his life and much of his own money to the restoration of Lew Trenchard Church, he had nothing but scorn for the work done by the others elsewhere.

The ironic use of inverted commas when speaking of the 'restoration' of other churches earned him many enemies, a fact for which he cared little or nothing. Among his fellow clergy he was as out of place as an eagle among barn-door fowls, and he seldom troubled to attend either chapter meetings or any of those social and pious gatherings which can so easily occupy a large part of a parson's time.

The Rector of Lew Trenchard

His output of work continued to be enormous. As his physical energy slowly declined, his mental activity if anything increased. Yet it is part of the strange paradox of his character that he was genuinely convinced all his life that he was so delicate that he was fully justified in spending many months away from his parish whenever he felt the need of a change of scene. This was not just self-indulgence; in part the habit may have grown from his early wanderings, and certainly his restless, inquisitive mind contributed to it. He may have felt, too, a deep-rooted dread of the return of the lung trouble from which he had suffered in youth.

Sabine's many-sided, dynamic personality earned him the respect of those who knew him intimately, but these were few, for he made friends slowly, caring little for the companionship of those with whom he did not share some intellectual interest. Once formed, however, his friendships were constant and enduring, and among the little band of enthusiasts who worked with him at the archaeological exploration of Dartmoor and the Cornish moors, or that other little group who shared his countless expeditions in quest of the dying folk-music of the Westcountry, he was always the friend and leader (see chapter 10).

In Lew Trenchard itself he is scarcely remembered for any of the things for which he was famous during his lifetime. Rather he is the man who caught boys robbing his orchard and, after reprimanding them, had a basket of eating apples placed regularly at his back door so that they should never again be tempted to steal. He is the parson who each autumn visited every house in his parish to leave a gift of bulbs, calling again without fail the following spring to see them in bloom. He is the man who drove the twenty miles to Okehampton and back in his open dog-cart to give a birthday present of sweets to an ex-choirboy who was at school there; the man who distributed a present of coal each Christmas to every cottage on his estate. There are

The Rector of Lew Trenchard

still those who love to recount stories of his personal kindness, his peculiarities, and his periodic outbursts of impatience, for he was always in a hurry and loathed to be kept waiting by anyone, whether parishioner or visiting bishop. 'Usually I absolutely loved him,' said one who remembered him very well indeed, 'but there were times when I hated him.' This remark, from someone who knew him intimately, confirms him as one of those people who can be loved, admired or even detested, according to one's nature and outlook, but who cannot be ignored.

8

The Squarson

When Sabine first inherited the Lew Trenchard estate in 1872 it was not very much to be proud of, and in this it resembled the majority of similar small estates in the country. The soil of east and south Devon is of high agricultural quality, capable of carrying heavy crops; the climate, too, is on the whole ideal for mixed farming, being mild and sunny, while seldom becoming either too hot or over-dry. This is the 'Red Devon by the Sea' of the song-writer and the tourist's imagination; a land of fat cattle, great apple orchards and prosperous farmers. But unfortunately north and west Devon are less favoured. Exmoor and Dartmoor possess a wild beauty of their own, but they have broken the heart of many a man who tried to cultivate them. Dartmoor in particular is wild, desolate and swept in winter by storms that wash away all traces of fertility. Even away from the moors much of the soil is cold and stiff to work and the rainfall is apt to be too high for successful arable farming. As in the Highlands of Scotland oats were the staple diet of the people for centuries: 'You men of Devon are little better than horses,' commented an irate medieval baron.

The soil at Lew Trenchard is mostly somewhat better than

in the north of the county, but on the whole the same agricultural pattern prevails. It is a land of small farms, many little larger than smallholdings, from which the squires in their day drew small rents. Even before the repeal of the Corn Laws there was no great agricultural prosperity. The estates of the 'landed gentry' were small compared to those of the great squires in more wealthy areas and the Devon squirearchy, even in its heyday, never had the money to build stately mansions. The few modest if lovely old manor houses dated from the days when Devon led the world in maritime adventure; and some pretentious houses of much more recent date were built to enhance the grandeur of newcomers to the county, whose wealth originated not from the land but from industry or the Stock Exchange. With this meagre background, Sabine set himself a formidable task when he determined to make all the houses on the estate comfortable and sound, including his own. Just how urgent was the need can be judged from his account of the state of one of the cottages, given in his novel *Arminell*; in his *Reminiscences* he mentions that the cottage described was in reality the keeper's cottage at Lew Trenchard when he first knew it. The account does not mince matters, leaving a grim picture of revolting squalor; and, incredible as it may seem, it was in the basement of this sodden, rat-infested hovel, that, before his return, the weekly Sunday School was held.

Several of his other farms and cottages were almost equally dilapidated and ready money was urgently needed.

To add to his difficulties, Sabine returned home at an inauspicious time, for the unpredictable English climate was yielding an unusually protracted spell of cold, wet weather. The year 1879 had been disastrous for British agriculture. The smaller squires were badly hit financially and from then onward were increasingly threatened by falling rents, mortgages, bank overdrafts and death-duties. It is only against this background that we can fully appreciate all the improvements that Sabine man-

The Squarson

aged to effect between his homecoming in 1881 and his death in 1924.

His father had not helped matters. His long spell of European wandering over, he had finally settled down at Lew Trenchard and done his best to improve the value of his property by opening limestone and slate quarries and mining manganese, but none of these ventures had proved a paying proposition. He also spent much time and money in designing and constructing agricultural machinery, but he was no Jethro Tull and his inventions for the most part obstinately refused to work, while his tenants with equal obstinacy refused to use those that did. So it was that Mary's first impressions of Lew Trenchard, when she came there in 1881 as a girl of twelve, were of fields scarred with derelict mining projects and littered with rusting farm machinery.

It was not from the rents that Sabine received as a landlord, nor from the small stipend that he earned as rector of the parish, that he managed in the course of years to bring up his enormous family, to rebuild his home, his farms and his cottages, and to remodel his whole property, but from the money he received from his books. If at times the quality of his work suffered, it was not so much because he did not take writing sufficiently seriously but because it was for him primarily a means to an end.

When first he inherited Lew House it was, like many Devon manors, a very unpretentious building; long, low, rectangular and rat-infested, the line of the front only broken by a glass porch. The walls, as was commonly the custom in such houses in Devon, were plastered over to protect them from the weather. Slowly as the years went by and money became available Sabine transformed it. He never employed an architect, preferring to depend upon his own judgment, and in consequence the result was original. There is no denying that it was a success, and it has about it a subtly continental flavour which one grows to associate with most of Sabine's work; the product of one who

The Squarson

had travelled much and kept his eyes open for whatever seemed to him admirable.

When writing of other people's homes, Sabine had a fund of derisive adjectives which he was over-fond of using: 'Cockney-Gothic' is a typical example. Lew House might equally well be described as 'Baring-Gould Tudor', though the epithet would certainly have infuriated him for though the general effect is that of an E-shaped Elizabethan house, it bears the unmistakable stamp of its designer's taste and personality. He had, for an amateur, an astonishing knowledge of old houses, of which he made a lifelong study and of which he wrote in such books as *An Old English Home* and *Old Country Life*, and this he put into practice as he went along, with what were on the whole amazingly satisfying results. Externally he remodelled the house and refaced the walls with local stone, pierced with granite windows. At one end a ballroom, at the other a library and in the centre a projecting porch, completed the traditional Elizabethan house of his dreams. A dream house it was, and in some ways he lived in a dream world of his own imagination. Nothing shows this more clearly than the fact that, as a final touch, he proudly erected over the front door a granite slab bearing the date 1620, which he had taken without remorse from 'Orchard', another old house on his estate. Others might have done the same, but who else would have shown the final result to his son-in-law, Harvey Dickinson, and said in absolute sincerity: 'It is lovely to be living at last in a genuine seventeenth-century house.'

Internally, too, Lew House was completely reconstructed. The rooms were lined with oak panelling throughout. A little of this was probably original; some is said to have come from farms that he was modernising and reconstructing at the same time, some he even picked up on the Continent during his many expeditions abroad; but most of it was frankly copied. The noble carving round the fireplace in his new ballroom came from Germany and Sabine was so shocked at the sum, far beyond his means, that he had impulsively paid for it that he hid it away for some time before he dared to show it to his wife—Grace had been raised in the hard school of poverty and had small sympathy with his periodic outbursts of extravagance.

Two houses in particular influenced him in his reconstruction of Lew House. The first was Sydenham, the beautiful old manor house in the neighbouring parish of Marystowe. The second was Dunsland, the family home of his son-in-law, Harvey Dickinson. One wing of Dunsland dated from the early seventeenth century and, though less beautiful than Sydenham externally, it contained much of its original oak panelling. Some of the panelling that Sabine had made for Lew House was obviously copied—and excellently copied—from this. The rooms in the late seventeenth-century wing of Dunsland were on the other hand lined with large, finely moulded panels of painted pine. These Sabine also greatly admired. On 28 November 1897 he wrote to Mary: 'Tell Harvey I was so delighted with the moulding of the panels at Dunsland that I copied them and am reproducing them in the ballroom here.' Dunsland, which eventually became the property of the National Trust, was completely destroyed by fire in November 1967. Nothing now remains to recall its appearance but a few photographs and the Lew panelling.

Sabine may at times have been careless in his writing, but over building matters he was a perfectionist. Any work that failed to reach his high standards had to be taken down and done all over again, no matter what it cost. This applied not only to his home but to all the work that he undertook in connection with the parish church and the other buildings on the estate. On one occasion one of Sabine's numerous young grandsons said innocently to a builder working at Lew: 'Oh, Mr . . ., you must be very rich. You are paid to do everything twice.'

Never at any time had he the slightest idea of how he stood financially. He would stride into his bank in Tavistock and catch

The Squarson

the eye of the nearest clerk: 'Tell me, boy,' he would say, 'have I any money left to pay my bills?' The young men always thought he was joking, but he was completely in earnest, for at a period when the majority of Englishmen considered saving to be a primary virtue, money was to him something merely to be made and spent. Nor was this all; despite his withering pen and ironic tongue, there was a very kindly side to his nature and he could never bring himself to believe harm of anyone whom he employed. Most of those who worked for him responded magnificently, but there were others who undoubtedly made a very good thing indeed out of the reconstruction of Lew House and the rest of the building work.

Again we are confronted with a seeming contradiction in his character. Despite his political views, his upbringing and his veneration for the past as he understood it produced a certain aristocratic outlook on life; but it was aristocracy in the high tradition that accepted to the full all its responsibilities as well as its privileges. To him the squire was an essential part of the village community, its head and natural leader, and it is perhaps significant that he is still remembered in Lew Trenchard as 'the Old Squire' and not 'the Old Rector'. But it went far deeper than this. His tenants and parishioners were not only his employees and his flock, and as such his responsibility, they were his friends and his relatives.

He never denied that rigid social barriers did commonly exist between the manor, the rectory and the village, but he always contended that this snobbery was of comparatively modern growth and was seldom if ever characteristic of the genuine manorial families who had owned the land for centuries. There had been a time when the small squire, so typical of Devon, had lived by farming the home farm himself and the parson had farmed the glebe. They then had common interests, a common outlook and a strong sense of belonging to a community.

The sons and daughters of the manor, the rectory and the

The Squarson

farm frequently intermarried, especially in the more remote parts of the country. It was the Industrial Revolution, the improvement of roads, the coming of the railways and, above all, the purchase of landed estates by newcomers whose fortunes had been made elsewhere, that changed the pattern of rural life and accelerated the social cleavage that had already begun a century before.

Many of the industrial towns were of so new a growth that wealthy business men could, like John Galsworthy's Forsytes, remember the yeoman stock from which they sprang. As a natural consequence, as soon as anyone had made a fortune in the town his first impulse was to return to the country; to become 'a man of property'; to acquire an estate where he could live what he deemed to be the life of a country gentleman. But in many cases he brought with him from the town that evil legacy of industrialism, the barrier between employer and employee. There were always estates to be had. The Civil War, drink, gambling, the attempt to live up to standards higher than the land could maintain, the abolition of the Corn Laws, and ever-increasing taxation and death-duties, ensured for each generation a continuous supply.

So at least Sabine thought, and in his book *Old Country Life* he took great pains to show the ties of blood that existed between the genuine old county families and their neighbours in the village, using church records and family pedigrees to prove his point. The squire's eldest son might marry the daughter of a peer, the younger daughter might wed the village blacksmith, and all was well. Only when one or other of them was guilty of some misconduct was the name struck out of the family pedigree. He emphasised, too, the fact that in the seventeenth century the domestic servant was treated as, and indeed often was, a member of the family and that it was not until the nineteenth century that she was relegated to the attic and the basement. Samuel Pepys in his diary for 12 November 1660 mentions that he took his own sister as servant in his house, and Sabine again quoted examples from the church registers of Devonshire parishes to show that this was quite commonly done.

These views explain at least in part not only Sabine's unpopularity with the fox-hunting squires among whom he lived and with the reactionary Church dignitaries under whom he served, but also the unusual way in which his own children were brought up. In that age of snobbery, when it was considered 'ladylike' for girls to do little more than play the piano and look decorative, and for young men to enter only the 'gentlemanly professions' of the Army, the Church and the Law, Sabine expected his sons to earn their living from an early age at any job that was available. He also insisted that his daughters should be useful as well as ornamental, though as every one of them married young, none of them had to earn her living for long.

Margaret was sent to study art in London, where she became friendly with Clara Butt, later the world-famous singer. She had real talent, but Sabine chaffed her unmercifully about what were in those days considered her modernist tendencies. In a book of family limericks, which unfortunately seems to have vanished, he wrote:

> There was a young person called Daisy,
> Whose ideas upon Art were quite crazy.
>   She dashed about paint
>   Saying 'Isn't it quaint,
> The Impressionist School of the lazy'.

Felicitas was also sent to London, to train as a hospital nurse, while Mary, who lived at home until her marriage, was responsible for all the sewing and mending; a formidable task in so large a household. All her life Mary loathed cooking, but she was an expert and indefatigable needlewoman. When not sewing she was knitting, a handicraft which she performed with such effort-

The Squarson

less ease that she could read aloud to her family while knitting the most complicated garment. She kept it up all her life. As an old lady she was nicknamed 'the Woolly Queen' and her only objection to church-going was what she considered the absurd convention that she must not knit during the sermon. The young Baring-Goulds indulged in a form of humour that led them to tell with deep gravity the wildest stories about one another in the hope that some unsuspecting visitor might one day believe them. One story about Mary was that she once went to bed with a ball of wool and woke up with a pair of socks.

Just how strong was the class prejudice and how narrowly the social barriers were drawn at that time can be gathered from a story Mary used to tell. She had been chaperoned to a dance by a particularly snobbish old lady who insisted on inspecting her programme of dancing partners. These included a young and penniless doctor who had recently set up his plate in the district. 'Cut it at once,' her mentor ordered. 'I certainly shall not,' retorted Mary. 'Papa would be furious with me if I did anything so rude.' On another occasion, a social gathering she attended with her mother, the talk turned, even then, on the difficulty of obtaining domestic help. Grace Baring-Gould had a fund of dry Yorkshire humour: 'It all depends on the way you treat your staff,' she remarked. 'I always give my sewing-woman one day off a week to go hunting.' Thirty years later Mary could still chuckle at the impact of her mother's remark upon her hearers. They threw up their hands in dismay. 'My dear,' they twittered, 'whatever does she look like on horseback?' 'Quite charming,' replied Grace, smiling across at her daughter.

Designing and constructing buildings, which began for Sabine as a duty, became an ever-increasing passion as the years went by. Not only did he restore his church, rebuild his home and remodel his farms and cottages, he continued to add to their number, saying as an excuse for the expenditure that it not only

The Squarson

gave employment to a number of craftsmen, but would one day help to house his unmarried daughters after he had gone. The cottages still stand, but not one daughter was left a spinster.

His hatred of ugliness also drew Sabine into trying his hand at landscape gardening on a large and costly scale. When first he inherited the property there was, almost at his front door, a huge and unsightly quarry, some 200 yd long and 80 ft deep, a relic of his father's activities. Nothing shows more clearly how unlike one another Sabine and his father were. Edward Baring-Gould was a product of the hard-headed age in which he lived, and this great limestone quarry had been only one of his many attempts to move with the times. Had it been coal and not limestone that lay buried beneath his land he would no doubt without remorse have produced a small edition of the Black Country. Instead, after growing to huge proportions, the quarry was finally abandoned, to remain a dangerous and disfiguring sore on the landscape. To Sabine this was intolerable. He could not refill it with stone, so instead he deflected a stream into it and produced a beautiful if somewhat sinister lake, with a little waterfall cascading down a 40-ft cliff on its northern side. The sloping southern side he planted with trees, and to complete the picture he built beside it a house which he named 'Rampenstein', later reduced to 'The Ramps'. Here for many years lived his last curate and successor, the Rev Gilbert Arundell.

At the foot of the tree-covered slope on the southern shore of the lake Sabine built a boat-house, designed in the style of a Swiss chalet, and above the door was inscribed the following chronogram, written by the Rev J. M. Gatrill:

   thy breaD upon the Waters Cast
   In CertaIn trust to fInd
   sInCe Well thou know'st God's eye doth Mark
   Where fIshes eyes are bLind.

The Squarson

Taking the figures represented by the Roman letter-numerals and reading X(10) for W, this curious device adds up as follows:

D (500), W (10), C (100), I (1), C (100), I (1), I (1), I (1),
C (100), W (10), M (1000), W (10), I (1), L (50) = 1885

This seems to suggest that the building of the boat-house, and so presumably the flooding of the quarry to form a lake, was completed by 1885, only four years after Sabine's return to Lew Trenchard as rector.

At one time he seriously considered the possibility of reflooding much of the valley below his house in order to restore the lake from which Lew is said to have derived its name, and he was still planning and carrying out alterations to his house and property when, at the age of eighty, the first World War finally put a stop to his building activities. He found great satisfaction in watching his dreams slowly coming true. One lovely summer evening he was standing in the porch of the house that he had rebuilt, gazing across the woods that he had replanted and beautified with flowering shrubs to form a setting for his lake, when he turned to his daughter Mary and quoted the words of the Sixteenth Psalm: 'The lot is fallen upon me in a fair ground. Yea, I have a goodly heritage.' He had indeed made it so and in doing it he had done something finer and deeper than the mere outward results showed, for he had restored to a number of men that pride in their work that makes the true craftsman. Had he done nothing else, this would have made his life worthwhile.

It has been his lot to be praised or criticised, perhaps overpraised and unduly criticised, for almost everything that he did in his long and busy life. His novels, his hymns, his theology, his work as an antiquary and as a collector of folk-songs, the style in which he rebuilt his home and the way in which he restored his church, have all brought him a popular admiration and have all been subject to expert attack, for he was by nature a populariser rather than a pedant, one who was essentially the

The Squarson

enthusiastic amateur of a hundred subjects rather than the complete master of one. Yet his work in encouraging local craftsmanship has been almost entirely ignored or forgotten. For none of his building activities did he ever import outside labour of any kind, for he was convinced that the village craftsmen with proper encouragement were capable of producing really first-class work.

Sabine's acquisition of part of the ceiling in the long gallery at Lew House would be considered by his critics as another typical action by 'this man with a magpie mind' as he was once called, but we can only examine the facts and form our own judgment. There stands in North Street, Exeter, a fine seventeenth-century building. When the street was widened the owner, Mr Mansfield, was compelled to remove the façade of his house, including part of the decorated ceiling of an upstairs room. Sabine immediately made an offer for it; he had it carefully sawn into sections and brought to Lew House on a farm cart, where it served as the basis and model for the plaster work in the whole gallery. The remainder still stands at 38 North Street, Exeter.

With this one exception, the moulds for all the ornate ceilings which are a feature of Lew House were made by the local carpenter; the plaster work was done by the estate masons; the wrought-iron gates were the work of the village blacksmith; all to Sabine's own designs. This has produced one curious result. Wherever he went, Sabine habitually filled notebooks with sketches of architectural designs that interested him. The plaster work in the ballroom contains much of what is said to be Masonic symbolism, a fact that has given rise to the erroneous idea that Sabine was a Freemason: in all probability designs were copied from some other house, whose builder was a Mason.

Sabine took conscious pride in the skill of his workmen and was ungrudging in his praise of them. Of one he wrote:

The Squarson

> I had a young blacksmith who shod horses and did little more, nothing artistic. I took him about the country to show him old fine hammered ironwork, and then I drew him a design for my principal gates, and bade him execute it. He was fired with artistic zeal; and now, a middle-aged man, he does no other ironwork but what is ornamental and artistic, and for three hundred years hence William Roberts' gates will recall him.

Under the stimulus of his leadership and enthusiasm, local men again became the artists in wood and plaster, iron and stone, that they had been in former centuries. The materials in which they worked were mainly produced on the estate: the stone and slate were quarried locally, the granite for the mullioned windows came from the nearby moor, much of the timber from Lew Wood.

Lew House has matured and mellowed with the years, until it has become part of the lovely Devon landscape. One can only trust that Sabine's hope in connection with William Roberts' gates may hold true for the whole building and that it will remain for the next 300 years as a memorial not only to its designer, but to the workers who were able to turn his dreams into a reality.

9

A Lantern for my Christ

Though for the sake of clarity the three tasks that Sabine set himself have been taken consecutively, of course they went on side by side throughout his long sojourn in Lew Trenchard. The spiritual arousing of his parishioners was a slow, continuous effort; the rebuilding of his home, farms and cottages was a piecemeal undertaking covering many years, regulated by the amount of money that he had available at any one time, which fluctuated year by year in accordance with how well his books were selling. In the same way the restoration of the parish church could not be accomplished all at once. Here, Sabine had, or at least took, a completely free hand and he set about it, as he did everything else, in his own way. All the work, even the superb carving of the wooden screen and pulpit, was done locally, a little at a time, as funds became available; while the numerous ornaments that he installed were never new; he obtained genuine antiques, over the course of many years, by methods all his own and usually at his own expense.

Lew Trenchard Church, like so many others in Devon, is close to the Manor House with no other buildings near it; they mark the site of the original settlement, made in Saxon times

A Lantern for my Christ

or earlier, and the cottages of the villagers once clustered about them. The majority of those dwelling in the parish today either live in isolated farms or in comparatively modern houses and cottages along the A30 main road that borders the parish. In coaching days new hamlets tended to spring up along the newly macadamised main roads. Later, in many places, yet another hamlet grew up beside the railway station. Then with the decline in the rural population during the nineteenth century, it became quite usual for the cottages round the church and manor to disappear altogether. This is what happened at Lew Trenchard and in consequence some curious ideas have arisen, particularly among the many tourists. In fact a parish church has stood on this spot for more than a thousand years. Of the original building nothing now remains, nor have we any clue to what it looked like, for in 1261 it was completely rebuilt and re-dedicated to St Peter. Originally it had been dedicated to St Petrock, 'the captain of the Cornish Saints', the patron saint of a number of Cornish and Devonshire parishes like Padstowe, Petrockstowe and Newton St Petrock.

Of this second building in turn very little, if anything, remains for in 1520 the church was again rebuilt, this time in the late perpendicular style and in 1523-24 the interior was enriched with fine carved bench-ends and a carved rood-screen that survived for over three centuries. Ten years later, as previously described, Sabine's grandfather tidied up the church in accordance with the barbaric taste of the early nineteenth century. During the forty-eight years of Charles Baring-Gould's incumbency it slowly grew more and more dingy and neglected, and it must indeed have been a depressing place when Sabine first officiated there as rector.

Today it is visited by hundreds of sightseers every summer, who are drawn partly by curiosity, partly because Sabine is still remembered for his hymns, and partly to see its undoubted beauty, for it is in its own way a little jewel, though a very

A Lantern for my Christ

unusual one. It bears the unmistakable impress of Sabine's personality; and as would be expected of a venture for which Sabine was responsible, the result is wide open to expert criticism. To many visitors, it is oppressively cramped and cluttered. There is no denying, for instance, that the screen is extremely large for so small a church; but it is a genuine attempt to reconstruct the ancient one that it replaced—a water-colour drawing by the artist Condy, made before the destruction of the old screen, served Sabine as a guide. Overlarge or not, it is a magnificent piece of craftsmanship; the work of two sisters, the Misses Pinwell of Exeter and Ermington, who did all the carving in the long room at Lew House and are said to have used local oak throughout. The depth of the undercutting and the delicacy of the tracery are remarkable and place these two Victorian ladies among the master carvers of all time. However fine the sixteenth-century screen was, it is hard to believe that it was the work of finer craftsmen.

The fact that Sabine, in his *Book of the West*, speaks of the screen as a reconstruction from scraps of the ancient screen—those he saved in his youth for future use—has given rise to the idea that these scraps were incorporated in the new work, but this is not so. An inch-by-inch examination of the present screen shows no trace of antique wood. Originally the new screen was richly, perhaps too richly gilded, for Sabine had a passion for colour and the use of gold leaf which would have appealed more to the craftsmen of the Middle Ages than it does to us today. The gallery front of the screen contains eleven pictures from the Gospel story and twelve smaller ones depicting West country saints. A detailed description of them all is given in the church guidebook.

The pillar is cased in oak and the casing forms part of the rood-screen. It contains three niches, in one of which is a representation of St Petrock, the founder of the church; in the second stands St Peter, to whom the church was re-dedicated;

and the third holds a representation of St Michael the Archangel, to whom the north chapel is said to be dedicated. The pictures over the main portion of the screen, dividing the nave from the chancel, were painted by Sabine's second daughter, Margaret, and the remainder over the north aisle by Branscombe, a well-known West country artist. The work was begun in 1889, continued as money became available, and completed twenty-six years later, only nine years before Sabine's death. During half a century of neglect the pictures darkened and the gilding became so overlaid with grime and lamp-smoke that few realised that any of it had ever been gilded at all. The lack of colour and reflected light made the screen seem overpoweringly heavy for so small a church, a fact probably largely responsible for much of the criticism that it received. After a thorough cleansing the beauty of the pictures, the mellow warmth of the old gold and the delicacy of the carving were again revealed. The pulpit, which is modelled on the ancient pulpits in Launceston and Kenton churches, is another fine example of the work of the Pinwell sisters. Erected in 1900, it was paid for by Mr H. M. Sperling of Coombe Trenchard.

There is in the church much fine woodwork, old and new, but the real interest lies in the elusive yet faithful manner in which it mirrors the character of the man responsible for its restoration. On Sabine's tombstone in the churchyard are inscribed the words 'PARAVI LUCERNAM CHRISTO MEO' ('I have prepared a lantern for my Christ'). The epitaph was of his own choosing and expresses exactly what he tried to do when restoring the church he loved.

When one considers Sabine's continental upbringing and how the formative years of his life were spent, it is easy to understand why the subtly un-English atmosphere which is to be felt in Lew House is even more pronounced in the church. On his many trips abroad he ransacked Europe to embellish his restoration. There is over the altar a small stained-glass window above a large picture in a massive gilt frame, showing the Adoration of the Magi. The window, which is the work of Carl de Bouché of Munich, was not put in place until 1914. The picture is by Paul Deschwanden, a Swiss artist, whose religious paintings were at one time in great demand. On one of Sabine's many trips to Europe he had met the artist and admired his work. With his usual impetuosity he commissioned the picture with Lew Trenchard church in view, though it was not hung there till many years after its delivery in 1871, possibly because he was content to wait until he had obtained a stained-glass window of a suitable size to be placed above it. Lavidière's far better painting, of the Crucifixion, bought in 1868 on his honeymoon, has already been mentioned. It was hung in Lew Trenchard church thirteen years later. His impulsive purchases of things he admired did not always enhance his church, if only because some were too large for it. An example is the great brass altar cross, the history of which is now lost, though we know that the malachite stones set in it were given by Mrs Sperling as a thank-offering for recovery from a long illness.

The eagle lectern of gilded wood was turned out of a church in Brittany and somehow Sabine heard of it. It is said in an old guide book, probably written by Sabine himself, to have found its way to Lew Trenchard in 1905, but Arscott Dickinson was firmly convinced as a child that it was made of solid gold, and in 1905 he was a boy of twelve; so either he was singularly unsophisticated for his age, or the lectern reached Lew at an earlier date—another instance of Sabine's unreliability with dates. The magnificent brass chandelier in the chancel, which dates from the fifteenth century, came from the church of St Jacques, Malines. Sabine dashed across the Channel for it on hearing that the Belgian church was installing gas lighting and offering it for sale. It was placed in the church in 1880.

Germany, France, Switzerland, Belgium; Sabine ranged far to adorn and beautify his church in accordance with his taste.

A Lantern for my Christ

Whether he ever troubled to obtain a faculty for anything that he did should perhaps not be asked. In his early days he had fought fiercely with those set in authority over him, a trait that may well have had its origins in his youthful revolt against the authority of his autocratic father. When once firmly in the saddle at Lew Trenchard, he preferred to ignore authority altogether and simply do what he liked. Perhaps that is why on entering Lew Trenchard church today one feels again a certain awe, even a wistful envy, of this dreamer who was able to make his dreams come true and leave so strong a stamp of his own personality.

10

The Old Singing Men

Continual surprises await Sabine's biographer. A fresh anecdote, a newly discovered letter, or a previously overlooked passage in one of his many books, can completely upset any former mental image of the man. His steady work, after his return to Lew Trenchard, to accomplish the three objects that he had mapped out for himself has been examined; and he took his responsibilities as a parish priest so seriously that the 'spiritual arousing' of his parishioners must surely have ranked first in importance for him. No one reading his devotional books, written with such unquestionable sincerity, could doubt that this was so. And then in his last book, the second volume of his *Reminiscences*, he tells of his quest to save the Westcountry folk-songs from being lost for ever, and he writes with apparently equal sincerity: 'To this day I consider the recovery of our Westcountry melodies has been the principal achievement of my life.'

To some extent, no doubt, such a statement is an expression of humility, for at times he suffered deeply from the knowledge of how far he had fallen below his ideals. It was in this mood of self-questioning that he wrote in 1920 a moving letter to the village carpenter, Charles Davey, who for many years had been his churchwarden.

The Old Singing Men

My Dear Charlie,

I feel that from month to month my powers are failing me and that it cannot be for much longer that I shall be here. I write this to you because I sometimes feel so depressed, thinking of how little in my forty years as rector I have done for God and the souls of the dear Lew people.

But then, when most humbled I remember how that you, among others, have learned to love God and to serve Him with heart and soul and am comforted.

When I came here as rector forty years ago, I had two objects in view, to teach the Lew people to love God, and to be true to His Catholic Church. I feel deeply how little I have effected through my own shortcomings. But I trust that at the Last Day, when I stand in self-conscious humiliation before the throne of God, you and some others here will be able to speak a word for me.

I cannot express to you what a comfort and joy you are to me as a true servant of God.

So, dear Charlie, you see I lean on you as my advocate at the last.

I remain, yours very truly
S. Baring-Gould

Yet this is perhaps not the whole answer, for there were in his nature two overmastering passions, accentuated by his upbringing; passions that coloured his whole life and were reflected in everything that he did. They were his deep, some might say his exaggerated, veneration for the past and his delight in beautiful things. In consequence the saving from oblivion of the lovely, almost-forgotten Devon folk-songs satisfied his deepest instincts, for in doing so he was preserving things that were both old and beautiful. Certainly their collection gave him tremendous pleasure at the time and a great pride in retrospect.

Typically, he began almost accidentally the task that was to occupy many years of his life, giving him scores of tiring, uncomfortable journeys, and hundreds of hours of hard work. In 1888, he was dining with friends at the house of Daniel Radford, of

The Old Singing Men

Mount Tavy, when the conversation turned on Devonshire songs. Beyond 'Widdicombe Fair' and 'Arscott of Tetcott', a once-popular hunting ballad, no one could remember a single song in its entirety. Sabine wrote later:

> I remembered how when I was a boy I had ridden round Dartmoor and put up at little taverns.
> In them I had seen men sitting and smoking and heard them sing ballads. I mentioned this. My host said to me: 'Come, you are the man to undertake the job of collecting these songs and airs. It must be done at once, or it cannot be done at all, for in a few years they will be lost.'
> I shall not forget my walk back from Mount Tavy to Lew. My mind was in a ferment. I considered that I was on the out-start of a great and important work.

Two points strike one as astonishing in this passage. The first is the easy assumption that Sabine was the right man for the job, when in one all-important way he was completely unsuitable, for he had had no musical training whatever. The second is the energy of a man already over fifty who casually mentions that he preferred to walk and not drive home from Mary Tavy to Lew Trenchard; it was largely this restless energy that enabled him to save the folk-songs.

Having once made up his mind, he threw himself excitedly into the new task. Eventually he succeeded in making contact with the over sixty old men and three women singers, besides making many journeys on what proved to be false scents. But he was only just in time. Some of the old singers were already bedridden, while others were so bronchial that their cracked voices could hardly quaver out a tune. Others found it hard to recall the words of the songs of their youth. The 'Singing Men', or 'Song Men' as they were sometimes called, had in former years been in great demand in country districts, nowhere more so than in Devon, and had played an important part in the com-

The Old Singing Men

munity life of rural England, but times had changed and by the 1880s few people cared to hear them. 'Lord, your honour', one of them said sadly to Sabine, 'I haven't sung these thirty years. Volks now don't care to hear my songs. Most of 'em have gone right out of my head.' Worn-out, illiterate, these old men were the last remnant of that long line of bards, gleemen, jongleurs, troubadours and minstrels who had once been honoured guests in homes rich and poor, throughout the land; bitterly regretting that they had been so firmly laid aside, they warmed to the tall parson who still had an appreciation of their worth, and they were willing, even eager, to try to recall their songs for his benefit.

Like most old people they looked on the world through rose-tinted spectacles and regretted the passing of the life they knew and understood. Yet one unexpected fact emerges from a study of the Westcountry folk-songs. Farm labourers have never had an easy life; they have been throughout history among the lowest-paid and least-privileged workers in England. Yet the traditional songs that they loved to sing were often full of the joy of life and have few traces of the underlying bitterness that one might expect. Rather they mirror a high-hearted jollity, a broad, sometimes very broad, and incorrigible sense of the ludicrous, a joy in simple things, and a vindication of the lot of the countryman contrasted with that of the town-dweller. In *Old Country Life*, published in 1892, Sabine wrote:

> At Halwill in North Devon lives a fine old man, Roger Luxton, aged seventy-six, a great-grandfather, with bright eyes and an intelligent face. . . . The old man was very famous as a song-man, but his memory fails him as to a good number of the ballads he was wont to sing.
> 'Ah, your honour,' he said, ' in old times us used to be welcome in every farm-house at all shearing and haysel and harvest feasts. . . . All them things be given up. . . . The farmers be too grand to talk to us old chaps, and for certain they don't care to

The Old Singing Men

hear us zing. Why for nigh on forty years us old zingin-fellows have been drove to the public houses to zing.'

Some of the old men were sufficiently hale and hearty to visit Lew House and be entertained there. Sabine would make them comfortable beside a roaring fire in the hall with a tankard of ale beside them and coax them to sing song after song for him, noting down the words as they sang. With the tunes he had much more difficulty. All that he could do was to pick out the air with one finger on the piano and write it down, playing it back to the singer again and again until the old man was satisfied that he had recorded it correctly.

In their heyday some of the singing-men sang entirely without accompaniment, while others accompanied themselves on a fiddle, not held to the shoulder, but across the knee. One of these was William Huggins of Lydford, of whom Sabine was particularly fond. Another example of the singing-man at his best was James Parsons, an old hedger who lived on Lew Down, and was nicknamed 'the Singing Machine' because of his remarkable memory and seemingly inexhaustible repertoire, on which he would continue to draw night after night without ever repeating himself, provided that his tankard was regularly refilled. 'He was very strict with me,' wrote Sabine, 'and insisted on my taking down his airs correctly. "Thicky wi'n't do," he would say, "you've gotten that note not right. You mun know that I'm the master and you'm the scholar".'

Occasionally, when Sabine had visited an outlying cottage to learn some fresh song from an old man too frail to come to Lew House, he would drive home singing it over and over again in an attempt to keep the tune in his head until he reached his piano; if he always sang the song to the exact words that he had recorded it must in some cases have caused considerable surprise to any parishioner who overheard him. As the scope of his quest widened he found that his lack of musical training was making

The Old Singing Men

the task impossible, but the difficulty was overcome when he succeeded in arousing the interest of two collaborators, both expert musicians.

One was F. W. Bussell, of Brasenose College, Oxford, whose mother and sister rented 'The Ramps', the little house that Sabine had built beside the lake. Bussell, who later became a Doctor of Music and vice-principal of his college, spent his Christmas and long vacations at 'The Ramps' and went on many expeditions with Sabine in search of folk-songs. He was one of those brilliant eccentrics who add a flavour to life. He loved to sing in a high falsetto voice, entirely oblivious of the amusement he caused, and he dressed in the exaggerated clothes of a bygone age. Always he wore a hot-house flower in his button-hole, sent him specially from London. He would drive through the country lanes in a high-built vehicle of his own design, which enabled him to enjoy the view over the tops of the high Devonshire hedges but which periodically overturned whenever he became too absorbed in the scenery. He had too an unusual sense of humour that endeared him to Sabine, though his practical jokes and cultivated eccentricities belonged rather to the Regency period than the late Victorian age in which he lived. He once travelled in state across Europe with his mother, under the titles of the Baron Frederick von Rampenstein and the Dowager Baroness von Rampenstein, and succeeded in getting away with it. He was in fact an oddity and Sabine loved and collected oddities.

Sabine's other helper, to whom he owed even more, was a man of very different type. The Rev H. Fleetwood Sheppard, ten years older than Sabine, was an authority on sacred music, especially plain-song, and as Precentor of Doncaster Choral Union was recognised as one of the pioneers of improved church music. Sabine knew himself lucky in enlisting Sheppard as a collaborator. He always resented the fact that some of Sheppard's arrangements were omitted from the final edition of *Songs of the*

The Old Singing Men

West to make room for fresh material collected by Cecil Sharp, under whose musical editorship it was published. The subject cropped up in conversation one day when he was visiting his eldest daughter at Dunsland. The old man, as he then was, insisted on Mary going to the piano and playing through a number of the songs, first in the original edition and then in the Cecil Sharp edition, while he hummed the tunes and afterwards expressed himself very forcibly on what was still a sore subject.

In their search for genuinely traditional folk-songs, Bussell, Sheppard and Sabine would occasionally set out all together, and a strange trio they must have made: the tall hawk-faced Sabine, Sheppard, the gentle old musician, and Bussell, the little Oxford dandy. They would stay at wayside taverns and lonely moorland inns, entertaining such old men as could hobble so far and noting down their songs. They would pick their way along muddy, deeply rutted lanes or scarcely defined moorland tracks in search of singers too old and crippled to leave their isolated cottages. Often they suffered considerable discomfort, returning to Lew in Sabine's trap, drenched to the skin, occasionally they ran into real danger, as when Bussell fell into a quaking bog on Bodmin Moor, but always their enthusiasm drove them on. Wherever they went the old singing-men made them welcome, pathetically overjoyed to find anyone interested in their store of tunes. But if the singers themselves always welcomed them it was not invariably so with their womenfolk. On one occasion they found at Princetown a decrepit old man, alone in a cottage, who sang song after song for them with immense gusto. When on the following day Sabine returned for another instalment, his way was barred by a grim-faced woman. 'What do you mean by coming here and getting my 'usband to zing his drashy old songs, when he ought to be preparing to meet his Saviour. No, you shan't see him. He is in bed and shall remain there. I've took his trousers away and burnt 'em.' For once Sabine had met his match and he never saw the old man again. Another from whom

The Old Singing Men

he collected a number of songs was Samuel Fone of Mary Tavy. The old man was bedridden but was able to read, so Sabine lent him a thick folio of Broadside Ballads to help him pass the time. This thrilled the old fellow so greatly that he proceeded to sing the songs at the top of his voice all night long, a performance that not unnaturally produced violent protests from his wife and daughter, who threatened to burn the offending volume unless Sabine removed it at once.

The search had the added zest of bringing Sabine closely in touch with men exclusively from the working class. Their common enthusiasm broke down barriers and a genuine and touching affection would grow up between them. Despite his somewhat formidable appearance Sabine had the gift of being able to inspire confidence in those he met. He had done so at Horbury Brig and he did it again in Devonshire.

Between 1888 and 1890 Sabine visited, or was visited by, the following old singers. The list has been compiled from a number of sources but is probably still incomplete. It does, however, serve to show the time and energy that he expended on this one subject alone and it must be remembered that it in no way indicates the numerous false scents that he followed or his countless unsuccessful journeys. Even with the improved roads and motor transport of today it would be quite a formidable undertaking.

The Old Singing-men

William Aggett, Chagford
William Andrews, Sheepstor
Matthew Baker, a cripple, Lewdown
William Beare
John Bennett, a labourer, Chagford
J. Benney, Menheniot, Cornwall
R. Bickle, Two Bridges, Dartmoor
W. Bickle, Bridestowe
Richard Broad, St Keyne, Cornwall
Peter Cheriton, a shoemaker, Oakford, nr Tiverton

The Old Singing Men

Moses Cleave, Huckaby Bridge, Dartmoor
George Cole, a quarryman, Rundlestone, Dartmoor
Jonas Crocker, Belstone
Thomas Darke, a labourer, Whitstone, Cornwall
James Dingle, Coryton
John Dingle, Coryton
James Down, a blacksmith, Broadwood Widger
Joseph Dyer, Mawgan, Cornwall
Samuel Fone, a mason, Mary Tavy
Matthew Ford, Menheniot, Cornwall
William Friend, a labourer, Lydford
Edmund Fry, a thatcher, Lezant, Cornwall
J. Gerard, Cullyhole, nr Chagford
S. Gilbert, an innkeeper, Mawgan, Cornwall
Roger Hannaford, Widdicombe-in-the-Moor
Richard Hard, a roadmender, South Brent
John Helmore, a miller, South Brent
John Hext, Two Bridges, Dartmoor
J. Hockin, South Brent
Roger Huggins, a mason, Lydford
William Huggins, a mason, Lydford
William Kerswell, Two Bridges, Dartmoor
Adam Landry, Trebarta, Cornwall
J. Libby, a coachman, Cornwall
Roger Luxton, a labourer, Halwill
John Masters, Bradstone
... Nancekivell, a quarryman, Merrivale Bridge
William Nichols, Whitchurch, Tavistock
James Olver, a tanner, Launceston, Cornwall
Anne Painter, Looe, Cornwall
James Parsons, a hedger, Lewdown
Anthony Pascoe, Liskeard, Cornwall
J. Peake, a tanner, Liskeard, Cornwall
William Rice, Lamerton
John Richards, Lamerton
Peter Sandry, St Ervans, Cornwall
Sally Satterley, Huckaby Bridge
Henry Smith, Two Bridges, Dartmoor
Suey Stevens, a charwoman, Stowford
James Townsend, Holne, Dartmoor

The Old Singing Men

John Voysey, a labourer, Lewdown
John Watts, a quarryman, Thrushelton
J. Webb, a mine captain, Belstone
Henry Westaway, Belstone
John Woodridge, a blacksmith, Thrushelton

In addition, Sabine and his friends took down songs from workmen engaged on the construction of the Burrator Reservoir on Dartmoor, from four unnamed miners at Zell in Cornwall, from an old miner at Fowey in Cornwall, from a very old man at St Enodor, Cornwall and also from an old blind man, James Coaker, whose memory had become unreliable. There were probably many others as well.

Richard Hard, song-man of South Brent. Formerly a road mender, when Sabine knew him he was a cripple, no longer able to go stone-breaking, and was living with his wife on £4 per annum. From him Sabine took down some eighty songs.

The Old Singing Men

Once collected, the songs presented yet another problem. What was to be done with them? The antiquarian in Sabine made him wish to see them preserved for future reference in their original form, and to this end he presented the Plymouth City Library with a manuscript copy of the songs, giving the original words, alternative versions and the airs as taken down by Sheppard, Bussell and himself. It might have lain forgotten for a long time had not Sabine been, besides an antiquarian, a journalist and born populariser. The urge that made him as a young schoolmaster delight his pupils with the 'Saga of Grettir the Strong' and in later years a popular writer and preacher, now made him long for these songs that he had grown to love to have as wide a public as possible. He therefore went to what have been considered unjustifiable lengths to placate Victorian

John Helmore, a song-man of South Brent.

The Old Singing Men

taste by rewriting a number of the words. He was not alone in this, for Fleetwood Sheppard wrote new lyrics for several of the songs that he considered had words unfit for publication. How far they were right in doing this must remain a matter for individual opinion. Some of the original words were obscene, though often wedded to delightful tunes; others were, by the time they came to Sabine's notice, little more than corrupt and meaningless doggerel; many had a down-to-earth outspokenness when dealing with the relation of the sexes and certainly did not hesitate to name a spade a spade.

The known effect of one of these latter upon a certain Victorian gentleman is some indication of what would have been the result had an uncensored edition of the songs been made public : finding himself unable personally to visit an aged singer of whom he had heard, Sabine asked this person to represent him and take down the words of a song not previously recorded. The ballad was a long one. As Sabine received it from his friend, the first verses were clearly and neatly written down. By the middle of the song the writer's hand was quivering with emotion and by the end of it the writing had become almost completely illegible.

A volume containing such songs would never have been permitted on the piano of any Victorian middle-class home, yet to have cut out all those with questionable words would have deprived the collection of many of its best airs. Occasionally even Sabine himself would flinch, though for his time he was not squeamish. When Sheppard took down the air of a song called 'The Mole Catcher' from J. Hockin of South Brent, Sabine did not record the words at all. Later he found that the song was contained in an early *Garland of Verses*, but that the words had been torn out of the copy in the British Museum Library.

There was good precedent for substituting new words for the original ones in such cases. Robert Burns, Sir Walter Scott and others had done the same thing. Burns altered the words of 'On

The Old Singing Men

a May Morning so Early' to 'The Waukrife Mammy' for inclusion in Johnson's *Museum*; Joyce in his *Ancient Irish Music* included a version of the song, but added that for several reasons the original words could not be presented to the reader; to the famous old ballad 'John Barleycorn' Burns added some six stanzas of his own; in later years Cecil Sharp found it necessary to modify the words of some of the songs he collected in Somerset and elsewhere. Yet for his alterations Sabine has as usual come in for much criticism. True, he was no Burns; yet had he left well alone, it is doubtful if *Songs of the West* would ever have become known to the world at large. For a few he wrote completely new lyrics; of others he published, to quote his own expression, 'much chastened versions', and these, oddly enough, have been criticised both for being over-chastened and for not being chastened enough. The song 'The Three Drunken Maidens' for example has been objected to, even in the modified form in which it appeared in *Songs of the West*, with its last verse rewritten. On one occasion when three of Sabine's younger daughters sang and mimed it at a village concert it created quite a local sensation.

In 1890, Sabine went further in his endeavour to make the songs better known. At his own expense he organised a tour of the principal towns in Devon and Cornwall, personally leading the concert party, which included the ageing Fleetwood Sheppard and Bussell's sister as pianists. Mary and other members of Sabine's family were included in the cast, and the programmes contained solos, duets, choruses, tableaux and dances, all in costume. They played in Exeter, Plymouth, Launceston, Tavistock, Dartmouth, Ashburton, Newton Abbot, Torquay, Totnes, Penzance and Redruth, besides giving concerts in a number of smaller towns and villages. From Mary's account they all enjoyed themselves hugely, but their reception was lukewarm. Their respectable audiences hardly knew what to make of songs so different from the Victorian ballads to which they were accus-

The Old Singing Men

tomed; financially the tour was a failure and Sabine was considerably out of pocket. The performance of the 'Dilly Song' was often greeted with laughter by Cornish audiences, a fact that puzzled Sabine until he discovered that the air was at that time popular as a hymn tune in the local Methodist chapels. Sabine's party were pioneers in a field so old that it was for the majority of the listeners something completely new, and they suffered the usual fate of innovators. But their efforts paved the way for the twentieth century's enthusiasm for folk-song and dance.

Songs of the West was first published in parts in 1889, and as one volume in 1892. It was not until 1905 that the final edition under the musical editorship of Cecil Sharp was published. But it is Cecil Sharp, then a comparative newcomer in the field of folk-song, who is today universally honoured as its rediscoverer and preserver. Even *The Oxford Companion to Music* speaks of him as being more than any other single person responsible for the salving of this national heritage; much space and a page of illustrations are devoted to his work in this direction, while only one passing reference is made to Sabine as one of the leaders of the folk-music movement in England. Yet Sharp was first attracted to folk-music by seeing and hearing six Morris dancers performing on Boxing Day 1899, at Headington near Oxford. This was ten years after the first publication of *Songs of the West*. Even then, beyond noting down some of the tunes from the concertina player, Sharp made no immediate use of his discovery, though in telling the story of the revival of folk-music he always spoke of the incident as the turning point of his life. It was not until 1904 that he published the first volume of *Folk-Songs of Somerset*, and not until he resigned his position as Director of Studies at the Hampstead Conservatoire in 1905 was he able to give his full attention to folk-song. He was certainly corresponding with Sabine for some time before this, for on 2 February 1904 he wrote a letter to the Folk-Song Society,

The Old Singing Men

which he had founded in 1898, but into which he was striving to put new vitality:

> In proof of the interest that is being aroused by your journal allow me in conclusion to quote a letter just received from the Rev S. Baring-Gould, the well-known collector and editor of Cornish and Devonshire songs: 'I am so grateful that at last the public is being roused to the fact that we have a body of fine traditional music. It is full late now to collect. All my old men are dead but one'.

In 1904 and 1905 Cecil Sharp became a regular visitor to Lew Trenchard and this resulted in the publication of the revised and final edition of *Songs of the West* in 1905 and in a book of *English Folk-Songs for Schools* which he produced in collaboration with Sabine in 1906. To meet the requirements of the Board of Education it was as usual found necessary to modify some of the words. Sharp had grave doubts as to how far such a step was justified, but in order to get the songs introduced into the schools he agreed reluctantly that the end justified the means. It was Sabine, who with his facile gift for writing verse was actually responsible for the necessary modifications, that as usual received the blame.

Sharp unquestionably did magnificent work. He was a highly trained musician, which Sabine was not, and was a specialist with an all-absorbing enthusiasm for and knowledge of his subject, which to Sabine was only one of many interests. His opinion naturally carried great weight in musical circles, while Sabine's carried none. But he was not the true pioneer of the present-day revival in interest in folk-song and dance. As in many fields of pioneer work the credit has not gone to the men who really blazed the trail, and Sabine in old age felt somewhat sore about it. In the revival of folk-dancing also Sabine was in the van, for at his instigation his daughter Joan taught traditional dances in Lew Trenchard parish for several years prior to her

The Old Singing Men

marriage in 1907, and it would be interesting to know if there is any record of the deliberate formation of a folk-dance group in any English village before that date.

One of the songs excluded from the 1905 edition of *Songs of the West* is perhaps worth recalling. It has words by Sabine, inspired by the local ghost stories that arose round the last man to be hanged in chains in Devon, a murderer called Welland. Set to a curiously haunting air, it shows traces of the macabre streak in Sabine's nature. He named it 'Broadbury Gibbet'.

> On Broadbury down the ravens croak,
>   The breezes shriek and groan,
> Now low, now high, the white owls fly,
>   As shadows in the moon.
> The cotton grass grows under me,
>   In tufts of silver white.
> I swing and sway throughout the day,
> I sway and swing all night.
>
> On Broadbury down my gibbet stands,
>   Just where the highways cross.
> It tells the moments, marks the hours.
>   With shadow on the moss.
> And I am like a pendulum
>   That swing and never stay,
> The Death Clock of a bad old world.
>   That cankereth away.

But of all the songs to which Sabine set fresh words there is one that should never be forgotten by anyone who today values folk-music—not for its poetic value, but as a tribute to the old song-men of Devon, written by the man who loved them, sought them out and took down the old songs, which otherwise would have been lost for ever. Sabine had one of them especially in mind, the man from whom he took down the tune to which his words were set. This was William Huggins, a mason of Lydford,

The Old Singing Men

who died in 1889. Two slightly different versions of the words exist; one in the first edition of *Songs of the West* and the other in *Old Country Life*. The tune of this song, which Sabine called 'The Last of the Singers', can now only be found in the original edition of *Songs of the West*, for like 'Broadbury Gibbet' it was excluded from the 1905 edition. It describes the old song-man going from cottage to cottage, singing and playing his fiddle, and ends sadly:

> I be going. I reckon, full mellow
> To lay in the Churchyard my head;
> So say—God be wi' you old fellow;
> The last of the singers is dead.

Despite the later misconceptions, his contemporaries were well aware that it was to Sabine and no one else that the chief credit for saving Westcountry folk-songs should be given. In a paper read before the Devonshire Association at Barnstaple on 25 July 1917, Charles H. Laycock said:

> It is true that a small collection of sixteen Sussex folk-songs was made in this way so long ago as 1843, by the late Rev John Broadwood and printed for private circulation, but nothing further seems to have been done in the matter until the close of the 'eighties. And the one who must be regarded as the pioneer in this important work is our brother Devonian and fellow member, the Rev Sabine Baring-Gould, who with his colleague, the late Rev H. Fleetwood Sheppard, began to systematically collect and note down songs and ballads from the mouths of the people of Devon and Cornwall in 1888.
>
> Not we alone in the West Country, but indeed every true Englishman, owes him the deepest debt of gratitude for being virtually the first to bring to light the hidden treasures of folkmelody, which had for centuries been in the sole keeping of a small and much despised community and would almost certainly have been irretrievably lost to the world, had he not taken the matter in hand when he did.

The Old Singing Men

Today, when folk-song and dance are valued over much of the world, the subject of international gatherings and television programmes, it should be remembered that the English branch may be said to have begun in 1890, when Sabine took his little group of amateur singers and dancers on tour through Devon and Cornwall.

11

The Man of Letters

During his lifetime Sabine Baring-Gould was of course chiefly known to the outside world by his hymns and his books, for though he was not a recluse he mixed very little in the literary life of London or in such local society as Devonshire provided. Small talk bored him to distraction and he would retreat from a social gathering at the earliest moment good manners would permit, sometimes indeed considerably before, and bury himself once more in his library.

When he left his parish, as he frequently did, it was not often for the purpose of meeting people. He much preferred to tramp the high moors, measuring, mapping and musing on the relics of the past, either alone or in the company of a few chosen friends of similar taste. Just as in the collection of folk-songs Fleetwood Sheppard and Bussell were his constant companions, so many of his long tramps across Dartmoor were shared by his great friend Robert Burnard of Plymouth, who was equally interested in its antiquities. London was to Sabine a dreary place to which it was necessary to go periodically in order to visit the British Museum Library or to interview publishers. His interest in the Church of which he was a member was largely confined

The Man of Letters

to its history and doctrines. His pastoral work was limited to the care of his own few parishioners, for whom he retained a strong sense of responsibility.

In the wider field of Church work he took small part, nor was he encouraged to do so by his ecclesiastical superiors, most of whom had at one time or another suffered from his outspoken comments. The *Encyclopaedia Britannica* never spoke of him as being more than a novelist and in the 1969 edition has omitted any reference to him at all, even in connection with 'Onward, Christian Soldiers', which is mentioned as a hymn by Sullivan.

The puzzle of where he found the scholar's library that must have been absolutely necessary for his earlier theological writing, when he lived at Dalton and East Mersea, has already been considered. After he settled at Lew Trenchard he accumulated a very fine library of his own, containing many rare books by foreign authors which his early upbringing permitted him to read in the original. With a curate to help in his parish, he was freer than ever to make constant visits to public libraries, but the problem of how he found time for such a quantity of writing still remains. His work as rector, even of so small a parish, the personal superintendence of all the building work constantly being carried out on the estate, his habit of foreign travel, his voluminous reading and the long hours spent in research, his many expeditions by train, dog-cart and on foot to visit his old singing-men, the recording of their songs, his heavy correspondence, his countless journeys to Dartmoor, involving as they did long, unrecorded tramps through bog and heather to some of the most isolated spots in all Britain, would have filled any ordinary man's days and left little if any time for serious writing. Nor had he any of those aids to swift and easy writing now essential to an author: he never used a typewriter or even a fountain pen—every word was penned in his minute, meticulously tidy handwriting. At one time he had listed under his name in the catalogue of the British Museum Library more books than any other

The Man of Letters

English author, so many indeed that like other prolific authors he was unjustly suspected of employing 'ghosts'.

He was a very early riser and every day from early morning until late at night he was constantly occupied. No one who remembers him can ever recall having seen him relaxed in an easy chair. Men who work as hard as this are apt to burn themselves out by middle life, but he seemed to thrive on it. Through his ninety years of life his zest for acquiring unusual information and his urge to record his findings on paper never flagged. Strong as was his mind, his feet must have been even stronger, for he never sat down to write, but stood the whole time at a specially constructed desk. This was placed beside the great mullioned window in his library and here he stood, hour after hour, with the sun pouring down upon him and with his garden always in sight whenever he cared to raise his head.

To his friends and relatives Sabine frankly admitted that fiction was the branch of literature that appealed to him least and that he wrote novels largely to earn the money for projects that interested him far more. As already pointed out, the rebuilding of Lew House together with the farms and cottages on his estate would have been impossible had he not, in the twenty-five years between 1880 and 1905, had some forty novels accepted for publication. He would become restless and irritable until the outline of the new story began to take shape in his head. At such times he would suddenly abandon everything and vanish for the day, returning late in the evening after a long, solitary tramp across Dartmoor, quite himself again and ready to start writing on the following morning. He always had to force himself to begin a new novel, because doing so distracted him from writing something else which seemed to him of far greater value.

Although even his detractors, including J. M. Barrie, rated him among the ten best novelists of his time, posterity has never considered him to be a consistently first-rate writer of fiction.

The Man of Letters

But many of his novels do contain a remarkable atmosphere of the district in which they are set.

Mehalah, 'that remarkable Victorian novel', as the *New Statesman* called it when quoting from its description the nature of the district over which the great inundations of the sea occurred in 1953, was a story as fierce and untamed as the east winds that sweep the Essex coast in winter. *In the Roar of the Sea* (1892), a book still popular in Cornwall, carries with it something of the force and grandeur of the great Atlantic surges that batter the north Cornish cliffs. In *The Broom Squire* (1896), the scenery of the Surrey downs is more than a mere background, as are the Welsh mountains in *Pabo the Priest* (1889). *Grettir the Outlaw* (1890), a free translation of the *Saga of Grettir the Strong*, which was largely written for young people and was told in all probability in much the same words as Sabine used when he told it, chapter by chapter, to his young pupils at Hurstpierpoint School many years before, reflects vividly the wild, barren Icelandic scenery which had impressed him so strongly.

But it is in *Red Spider*, perhaps Sabine's best novel after *Mehalah*, that this underlying interpretation of the local scenery as an integral part of the story is most clearly marked. The scene is laid in the parish of Bratton Clovelly, only a few miles north of Lew Trenchard. The plot, like that of many of Sabine's novels, is inclined to be thin, but the tensions of village life, in which everyone knows everybody else's business, are vividly depicted, as is the quarrel between two farmers, with its petty beginnings and serious consequences. The story ends with their reconciliation and the marriage of the heroine, daughter of the village carrier, to one of the farmers. The slender plot is redeemed by powerful characterisation, and the way in which the countryside itself plays its part in the construction of the story is in some ways reminiscent of Thomas Hardy's 'Wessex' novels, although Sabine once admitted to Mary Dickinson that he was ashamed to say that he had never read any of Hardy's novels, since he seldom found time to read fiction of any kind, though he greatly admired Hardy's poetry. A glance at what remains of his library at Lew House shows that his real interest lay in books dealing with philosophy, travel, history, theology, essays and verse. Fiction is only represented by a few standard English classics like *Tom Jones* and *Vanity Fair*.

Red Spider was so well received that Sabine was induced to write the libretto of an operatic version of the story, and he was soon engaged in seeking a suitable composer with whom to collaborate. In an undated letter he wrote to Mary:

> Dearest Mary,
> When you are in Town . . . go and hear 'Hansel and Gretel' at the Princes'. I believe Humperdinck, the composer, is to be engaged to do my 'Red Spider'. . . .

Had Humperdinck been persuaded to compose the music, the opera might have been better known today, but it was eventually entrusted to Learmont Drysdale. Though completely forgotten today it was an immediate success.

Before the London production Sabine was confined to bed with a severe attack of influenza, but he insisted on sending Mary to coach the performers in the Devonshire dialect. After one completely exhausting day in which she failed dismally to teach the principal performer to say 'properly beautiful' with even the faintest suspicion of reality, she abandoned the task as hopeless and the cast were permitted to play their parts in the accepted 'Mummersetshire' accent of the London stage. This was probably just as well for the success of the opera, as the real Devonshire accent is—or was, for it is fast becoming much modified—very hard to follow unless the ear has been attuned to it. Sabine himself was never very reliable over the dialect words that he put into the mouths of his Devonshire characters. Being multilingual himself and not having spent his early boyhood in Devon, he was apt to use words and phrases that he had heard

The Man of Letters

in Yorkshire and Essex, just as he himself, as he freely admitted, used Danish or Dutch words when speaking German.

The provincial productions of *Red Spider* gave Sabine a wonderful chance to be on the move again, for he supervised many of them himself, writing to Mary to describe successful runs in Wales, Liverpool and Exeter, at all of which he was personally present. There were no doubt others as well. Of the Plymouth production he wrote:

Sept 2nd 1898

Dearest Mary,

'Red Spider' is a tremendous success and its luck is assured; crowded houses each night. Your tickets in Dress Circle are 49, 50, 51. You will have to go or send the money and the tickets will be yours. I doubt if there will be any left by this evening, as they are booked up very fast.

The performance was reviewed at length in the local papers and it is clear from their accounts that the story was slightly modified, as is customary in operatic versions.

Curiosity to see the first production of Rev S. Baring-Gould in a new department of literary effort, and the expectation of receiving an intellectual treat, filled the Theatre Royal Plymouth, last evening with an influential and representative audience to witness his romantic comic opera 'Red Spider', founded upon his novel of that title. Not only in his native county, but in all the counties of the English-speaking race, the rector of Lew Trenchard has long been known as a prolific and gifted writer in the realm of fiction; but as a dramatic author he comes before the public in an altogether new capacity. It was quite natural therefore that both the literary and play-loving public should be curious concerning his new venture, and his success as a novelist should arouse high expectations as to the quality and character of his work as a dramatist. It is perhaps no mean tribute to the merit of the opera to say that both feelings were abundantly

The Man of Letters

satisfied, as the audience convincingly testified by their rapt attention and frequent plaudits, and occasional demonstrations of enthusiasm. . . .

It is only necessary to add that the verdict of the audience was unmistakably favourable. From the first their sympathies were actively enlisted, and as the piece proceeded they grew more and more enthusiastic in their demonstrations of approval. At the end of the second act Mr Baring-Gould, who watched the performance from one of the boxes, was with the composer and principal artistes, called before the curtain. At the close of the performance the author was the recipient of another ovation. Acknowledging the compliment, Mr Baring-Gould said: 'I thank you for the kind way in which this opera has been received. Hitherto there have been operas, the themes of which have been Irish, Scotch, Italian, German and French subjects, but never an English one, and I hope and trust that this may be the beginning of a series of operas founded upon home English subjects.' With renewed cheers the audience dispersed to the strains of the National Anthem.

So much for the local press! If Sabine's speech was correctly reported, it is hard to understand why he so completely ignored the Gilbert and Sullivan operas, even if their themes are set less in England than in a curious, ironical dream-world of Gilbert's imagination. But that perhaps makes them particularly English. These excepted, *Red Spider* might be considered the forerunner of a number of truly English ballad operas, including Edward German's *Merry England*, Dame Ethel Smythe's *Bosun's Mate*, Vaughan Williams' *Hugh the Drover*, and Benjamin Britten's *Peter Grimes*, and Sabine has some claim to being a pioneer in yet another field.

Red Spider seems never to have been revived, either as a play or an opera, and the novel has long been out of print.

Sabine was always a little amused at the good reception accorded his novels, being far more concerned with the fate of the many religious and devotional books that he wrote. Despite his usual indifference to other people's opinion, the way in

The Man of Letters

which his *Lives of the Saints* was received was always a real disappointment to him. When he undertook the immense labour of writing it, he fully believed that it would be welcomed by Anglicans and Roman Catholics alike, but among Anglicans it met with a somewhat mixed reception and, because he dared to question the historical existence of some minor saints, it was placed on the Index by the Roman Catholics. In later years it was remembered with loathing by children of High Church clergy, who had suffered throughout life because they had been named after obscure and curiously-labelled saints unearthed by their fathers from Baring-Gould's *Lives*.

In all, fourteen volumes of Sabine's collected sermons were published and his graphic, journalistic style dates so surprisingly little, that, unlike most Victorian sermons, they are still readable.

Besides these, and tracts and essays, he produced some thirty religious and devotional works. Of these *The Origin and Development of Religious Belief* has already been referred to, but his most important book in this field was unquestionably *The Church Revival* at which he worked for many years and which was not completed until he was over eighty. It was his great contribution to the Church he served, for it set out to prove historically the unbroken thread of the Catholic heritage in the Church of England, which though weakened and distorted was never entirely lost. It is an outspoken, powerfully argued and very readable book, which suffers less than its companion volume, *The Evangelical Revival*, from occasional outbursts of that strong, if not violent, prejudice that was always part of his nature. Yet though he worked all his life to further the cause of the Catholic revival in the Church of England, he had considerable sympathy and understanding for the Evangelical point of view, and he openly admired much of what he found in Methodist churches, especially the hearty congregational singing.

The Man of Letters

Anglicanism in the mind of the general public, the Anglicanism to whose services the working man does not go, is represented by monotoned matins and evensong, the surpliced choir, hymns 'Ancient and Modern' and a sermon on domestic morality and the joys of the world to come. . . . Stand outside any little wayside dissenting chapel and listen to the singing. There is no organ, no choir—the congregation are choir and organ in one, and for heartiness they shame the service in the parish church.

Sabine could admire the bold, outspoken fighter in any cause, even when he totally disagreed with him. What he detested was 'the safe man' in Holy Orders, the cleric who has either no decided views of his own or is too timorous to state them. For the practitioner of what C. S. Lewis has called 'milk and water Christianity' he had little patience, whatever his denomination; for there must be, he contended, a direct and forthright teaching of doctrine and all that it implies.

The Church Revival was planned as part of a great history of the Church in England since the Reformation, and was first published in 1914. The Great War intervened; the costs of production rose enormously and the work was never published as a whole, but another portion, *The Evangelical Revival,* followed in 1920. The latter, though it contains much interesting scholarship, is more biased and less convincing than *The Church Revival* and in places shows definite signs that its author's mental powers were at last in decline.

In the course of his career as a writer, Sabine produced several biographies, including lives of Nelson, Napoleon and Nero, and a careless little masterpiece about another Westcountry parson, the Rev Robert Stephen Hawker, which he called *The Vicar of Morwenstowe.* Like Sabine himself, Hawker was the product of an age that permitted, even encouraged, individuality, and he was one of the most picturesque persons ever to be ordained a priest of the Church of England.

Born in 1804, he grew up in Plymouth and Stratton, of which

The Man of Letters

parish his father was vicar until his death in 1845. As a boy, Hawker was famous for a series of wild pranks, but he early showed literary ability and his first book of poems was published when he was only seventeen. At nineteen he entered Pembroke College, Oxford, but on hearing that his father could not afford to keep him there, Hawker immediately proposed to and was accepted by a lady of forty-one who lived at Bude and had a small fortune of her own. Once married, he returned to Oxford to complete his studies, with his wife riding pillion behind him on his horse. The marriage is said to have proved completely successful, and on the death of his wife at the age of eighty, he was heartbroken. In the following year however he consoled himself by marrying a lady many years his junior, and this marriage, too, seems to have worked out well.

Throughout Hawker's life, his piety, mysticism and poetic powers were only equalled by his extraordinary eccentricities. When vicar of Morwenstowe he would dress in sea-boots, a fisherman's jersey with a large red cross embroidered on the front of it and on top a purple cassock. This, he maintained, was the correct dress for a priest of the ancient Celtic Church, to which he claimed to belong. He was a scholar and an antiquary; his book *Footsteps of Former Men in Far Cornwall* anticipated much of Sabine's later work. Tennyson admitted that Hawker's long unfinished poem 'The Quest of the Sangraal' was superior to anything that he himself had written around the Arthurian legends. Hawker was also a humanitarian who fought the cause of the underpaid and underprivileged farm workers and he led a number of rescues to save the lives of shipwrecked sailors.

An early work of Sabine's was the volume entitled *Curious Myths of the Middle Ages*, published in 1866, and in 1868 a second volume followed. In these he retold a wide range of mostly well-known legends, like the tales of 'The Wandering Jew' and 'The Dog Gellert'. The books proved sufficiently popular to

The Man of Letters

justify their republication in a one-volume edition in 1869, the year in which also appeared his *Curiosities of Olden Times*, a little book containing a series of articles that ranged from 'Strange Wills' to 'Ghosts in Court'. This ran to several impressions and a new edition in 1895. In 1874 the collection in two volumes of *Yorkshire Oddities and Strange Events* appeared, followed in 1889 and 1891 by two series of *Historical Oddities and Strange Events*, the second being reissued in 1893 under the title of *Freaks of Fanaticism*.

In a short preface he wrote: 'An antiquary lights upon many a curiosity whilst overhauling the dusty tomes of ancient writers. This little book is a small museum in which I have preserved some of the quaintest relics which have attracted me during my labour'. But we are left in doubt as to how and where, while bogged down in 'Dalton i't Muck', he ever laid hands on those 'dusty tomes' from which he drew his material.

In 1908 and 1909 *Devonshire Characters and Strange Events* and *Cornish Characters and Strange Events* were published, each in two volumes. These books proved very popular, especially in the West of England, and a cheap edition of the former was reissued by the Bodley Head in 1926, two years after his death. Wrestlers, writers, inventors, murderers and eccentrics jostle shoulders: John Gay of 'Beggar's Opera' fame is here, and so is Sir Goldsworthy Gurney of Bude, who produced the oxyhydrogen light and illuminated the House of Commons with it, and who ran a steam coach service from Bath to London, two years before Stephenson's 'Rocket' was chosen for the Manchester to Liverpool Railway in 1829.

Here, too, is Anthony Payne, the giant retainer of Sir Bevil Grenville, of whom Hawker of Morwenstowe had previously written in *Footsteps of Former Men in Far Cornwall*; Dolly Pentreath, the last person to speak the old Celtic tongue of Cornwall; white witches; wife sales in Devonshire villages; and Lieutenant Goldsmith, RN, of the cutter *Nimble*, who in 1824

The Man of Letters

overthrew the Logan Rock at St Levan in Cornwall, but was made to replace it by the Admiralty at his own expense, unless he wished to lose his commission. In all they contain short biographies of sixty-two Devonians and seventy-nine Cornishmen.

In *Old Country Life* (1889), a book which ran to four editions in three years, and in *An Old English Home*, published in the same year, he recalls charmingly and somewhat nostalgically a rural England that was already dying out in his youth and of which few traces remain today. But of all the now nearly forgotten books that Sabine wrote, perhaps one of the most interesting and certainly one of the most revealing is his *Tragedy of the Caesars* (1892). This contains over 300,000 words and 117 illustrations. It ran to two editions in its original two-volume form and a third one-volume edition was published in 1895.

Sabine spent two consecutive winters in Italy, nursing his health and leaving the care of Lew Trenchard parish to his curate. How serious that weakness of the lungs from which he had suffered since boyhood really was, and how far these journeys were simply the outcome of his overwhelming mental and physical activity is impossible to say; but they brought him to a new and absorbing line of study. As he wandered through the Italian museums his attention was first arrested and then engrossed by the collections of portrait busts of the ancient Roman emperors. His wide reading had already told him something of these men, but he felt that here was something that the chroniclers and historians had failed to tell.

> To read Tacitus, Suetonius, and Dio in England and to read them looking up into the eyes of those whose acts were recorded, are two very different things.
>
> It seemed to me that the study of these faces helped me to understand the characters and personal histories of these Julians and Claudians in a way impossible apart from them, and explain many a psychological puzzle.

The Man of Letters

The outcome was a very readable book, crowded with a mass of information for which, as usual, he does not pause to quote his authority. For once however he does see fit to justify himself for this omission, saying that when first written the pages were crowded with references which he cut away as unnecessary, feeling that the scholar would know where to look for them anyway, and the general reader would only be put off by their insertion. He had in fact the good sense to avoid writing as the scientific historian he was not, but to be the scholarly master-journalist that he was, the man with a thousand interests and the uncanny knack of awakening a similar interest in others.

His unusual approach to the study of the Roman emperors was typical of his unashamedly prejudiced outlook on life in general. After long gazing at the portrait busts and statues, he formed from the sculptured features his own impression of the character of each. After that he wrote their histories in detail, but consciously or unconsciously these biographies had to be made to conform to that first impression. The case of Julius Caesar is a good example. Sabine was familiar with, and reproduced in his book, a dozen or more portraits of his hero, photographs of his statues and busts now scattered through the great European museums; seemingly the beautiful British Museum head impressed him most deeply. From a careful study of these there emerged in his mind an idealised Julius Caesar, of a character in keeping with features that would have done credit to an ascetic mediaeval bishop. Such a man, he reasoned, could not possibly have had a son by Cleopatra, and obviously the stories of his notorious profligacy in youth must have been disgraceful calumnies. The mind of the professional, scientific historian fortunately does not work in this way, but to understand Sabine at all we must accept the fact that his undoubtedly did.

His first book of travel, and in some ways his best, was

The Man of Letters

Iceland, its Scenes and Sagas, which has already been mentioned, and we have seen how he taught himself Icelandic in order to read its literature. In writing of other countries, his linguistic powers gave him the great advantage, denied to many wanderers, of being able to read and study without difficulty in the public libraries of the countries he described. During Queen Victoria's reign, the English reading public took a lively interest in Germany and its people and in consequence books about Germany had a ready sale. In 1879, Sabine wrote a two-volume work on *Germany, Past and Present*, which two years later was reissued in an abridged edition. This was followed by *Germany* in 1883, and by another book of the same name, written in conjunction with A. Gilman in 1886, for *The Story of the Nations* series.

The growing tension between England and Germany after the death of Victoria lessened the appeal of such books, and he wrote only two more on the subject: *A Book of the Rhine*, published in 1906, and *The Land of Teck and its neighbours*, published five years later. It must have been in connection with this book that he made a visit to London to call on the Duke of Teck, described in a letter to Mary dated 29 September 1910 as 'a very pleasant person'.

Sabine had however already written two books about France: *In Troubadour Land* (1891) and *The Deserts of Southern France* (1892). With the increasing friendliness fostered by King Edward VII and culminating in the *Entente Cordiale* of 1904, France became the country most frequented by English visitors and books about France and her history were increasingly in demand, a fact of which Sabine, with his unfailing journalistic flair, quickly took advantage. In 1901 *A Book of Brittany* was published, followed in 1903 by *Brittany*, written for the Methuen 'Little Guides' series. First attracted to Brittany by its wealth of stone monuments, similar to but far more numerous than those on Dartmoor, Sabine had grown to love the Breton fisher-folk

The Man of Letters

with their Celtic affinities to the Cornish, and when in 1902 they were faced with starvation, owing to a disastrous fishing season, he raised a fund for their relief, which was distributed by the British consul at Brest.

In 1905, he wrote *A Book of the Riviera*, a district then becoming increasingly popular among wealthy tourists, and in 1907 two more books about France were published: *A Book of the Pyrenees* and *A Book of the Cevennes*. By this time he was seventy-three, his foreign travels were over, and these were the last of his European guide-books. But meanwhile there was Britain itself needing to be written up.

Sabine the traveller wrote copiously of all the places he visited —guidebooks if you like, but what guidebooks, for they all mirror his insatiable curiosity and are bursting with legends and unusual facts.

In 1889, he had written *A Book of the West* in two volumes, dealing with Devon and Cornwall. This was followed by *A Book of North Wales* (1903), *A Book of South Wales* (1905), and another book on Cornwall, his last of this type, for the Cambridge County Geographies in 1910. In 1901 and 1902, when he had reached the late sixties, an age when most people need to take life more easily, his output of writing reached its peak. During these two years four novels, *Royal Georgie*, *The Frobishers*, *Miss Quillet* and *Nebo the Nailer* were published, besides the two books on Brittany, an historical introduction to a book on Bath, and a number of articles and short stories.

This torrent of writing is probably accounted for by the fact that about this time, as his letters to his daughter Mary show, he was very hard up, a state of affairs that was entirely his own fault, brought about by reckless spending on his rebuilding projects. He seems to have been in real danger of bankruptcy and for a time found himself in such straightened circumstances that he was forced to sell off all his horses and close Lew House. On 2 March 1901 he wrote to Mary refusing with thanks her

The Man of Letters

husband's offer to lend him a horse and carriage. Instead he transported his wife and unmarried daughters to France, where at that time living was cheap, and there for a while at least they lived in very humble lodgings.

England at the time of the Boer War had become unpopular with other European countries and in the poor district in which the Baring-Goulds lodged, the local children delighted to insult and pelt with filth Sabine's younger daughters as they walked to and from school to which they were temporarily attached. According to Joan's account, the girls in their turn were disgusted at the cruelty of the French peasants to their animals, especially when on market days poultry, lambs and calves were brought in for sale alive, to lie in the hot sun all day with their legs tied, without water and tormented by flies. The young Baring-Goulds were an outspoken lot and in consequence almost continuous quarrels ensued. To Sabine this must indeed have seemed a different Europe from the outwardly respectful and admiring one through which he had wandered with his parents as a boy.

Lew Trenchard parish, judging from the registers, was at this time left in charge of the assistant curate, the Rev W. J. Whitwell, though Sabine seems to have come home periodically. Eventually things righted themselves, but the financial crisis explains why Sabine at times wrote over-hastily and why he was so anxious that his sons should begin to earn their own living at the earliest possible age.

For the wild expanse of Dartmoor, that lay almost at his doorstep at Lew Trenchard, Sabine had a love that amounted almost to an obsession. Away from its few well-paved motor roads, the moor is still, for all its beauty, a desolate and lonely place. In Sabine's day it was infinitely more so. Yet there is scarcely a spot on its wide expanse to which his long legs did not at one time or another carry him. Alone, or in company with his friend

The Man of Letters

Robert Burnard, he examined, gazed upon and wondered at the many remains of prehistoric man; the hut circles, stone alignments, avenues and circles of standing stones that they had raised. If at times he jumped too easily to unjustified conclusions and if some at least of his conjectures have in part been discredited, it is only fair to remember that he was among the first to take any interest in them at all.

Everything about the moor fascinated him: the traces of the medieval tin workers, the ancient stone crosses, the legends, the simple life of the moormen, the lovely flora of bog and upland, the glorious air and the rugged scenery; and of them all he wrote enthusiastically in *A Book of Dartmoor, A Book of the West* and elsewhere. He also left us, in the guise of fiction, pen-pictures of the moormen whom he met, notably in a volume of short stories, entitled *Dartmoor Idylls*. His affection for Dartmoor had begun as a boy and for him it remained to the end of his life 'that region I love best in the world'.

Despite his large household and busy life he was indeed by nature a solitary man. When travelling, it was the wild places that drew him; the deserts of Southern France; the Black Forest of Germany; the lonely mountains of Iceland. In towns it was only the quiet buildings that attracted him, the ancient churches, the medieval guildhalls, the half-ruined castles, the museums and libraries, the places where he could gaze and ponder on the past.

So, at home, when he found the calls of everyday life becoming too insistent, when he had the plot of a new novel to work out, or when a book he was writing was not developing satisfactorily, he would call for his dog-cart and be off for a long day on the moors, to come back refreshed and invigorated. Dartmoor was his cure-all for the minor ills of life, not only for himself but for his family: if the children were ailing, it was not to a doctor, but to Dartmoor they were sent, that its pure air might blow away the germs. On the whole the system worked, for they were a hardy lot, though on one occasion Joan was packed

The Man of Letters

off to the moor to blow away a cold and returned with pneumonia.

It is not, however, in his books, but in back volumes of the *Transactions* of the Devonshire Association, of which he was president in 1896, that we find his most lasting and important work on Dartmoor. His presidential address, given at Ashburton, ranges over all that was then known of Paleolithic and Neolithic man, and settles down to his favourite topic of the prehistoric remains on Dartmoor. Between 1878, when he was first elected a member, and his presidency in 1896, his contributions to the *Transactions* covered a wide range of local history, folk-lore and dialect, mostly connected with the moor. He was for many years secretary of the Dartmoor Exploration Committee, appointed by the Association, and wrote their periodic reports.

It is with his work in connection with the antiquities of Dartmoor that Sabine's name is chiefly remembered today by antiquarians, but in fact he did a considerable amount of pioneer research in Cornwall as well. In 1892 he contributed a paper to the *Journal* of the Royal Institution of Cornwall entitled 'The Ancient Settlements on Trewortha Marsh'. In this he describes in detail a carefully organised 'dig', made possible in the previous year by the kindness of the landowner, T. R. Bolitho, and by F. R. Rodd, who placed his workmen at Sabine's disposal. Sabine's careful drawings and plans are reproduced in five accompanying plates, together with a mass of detailed measurements that seem to prove that on this occasion at least there was none of that lack of accuracy that has so marred the reputation of his work. In the following year he contributed another, shorter paper with two accompanying plates, describing further work undertaken at the same spot.

Over a number of years he compiled a long catalogue of saints connected with Cornwall, together with 'An Epitome of their Lives and a List of Churches and Chapels Dedicated to them'. It was in appreciation of this formidable task that the Royal

The Man of Letters

Institution of Cornwall elected him their president from 1897 to 1899.

His two presidential addresses contain some of his best historical work. For that of 1898 he took 'The Early History of Cornwall' as his theme, making a careful and scholarly comparison of Welsh, Irish and Cornish sources and tracing the history of the Celtic kingdom of West Wales, which had its capital at Exeter, until its final break-up after the campaigns of Athelstan in 926 and 928. Elsewhere, Sabine associated the site of the Saxon victory at a place called Galleford with Galford Down in Lew Trenchard parish and connected it with a field still called 'Battle Field'. It is a likely spot, though this has since been questioned.

So closely were the Cornish saints linked with the social and political life of their day that Sabine's address on the early history of Cornwall led naturally to his second one, given in 1899, on 'The Celtic Saints'. In this he set out to show that the Cornish 'saints', who were not canonised holy men but simply heads of early ecclesiastical settlements, stepped into the shoes of the pagan druids and bards, who were credited with supernatural powers. These, on request, would lay a curse on the wrongdoers, and were in Sabine's opinion the forerunners of the witches, who were dreaded in Devon and Cornwall even in his own youth for their power of 'ill-wishing' those who offended them.

In 1902, Sabine was presented with the Henwood Gold Medal, awarded every three years by the Royal Institution of Cornwall. In the following year, in conjunction with his friends Robert Burnard, The Rev J. K. Anderson and J. D. Enys, Sabine took a leading part in the exploration of Tregear Rounds, between Wadebridge and Camelford, one of the great earthworks that line the North Devon and North Cornish coasts. Urged on by his insatiable interest in the past, Sabine also became what might be described as the father of the risky hobby

The Man of Letters

of 'pot-holing'. Before the days of the electric torch he forced his way into a number of unexplored caverns, not only in England but on the Continent, especially in France.

Wherever men in former times had found refuge from wild beasts, from persecution, or the law, deep underground or on precipitous crags, we find Sabine trying to follow them and writing graphically of all he found in such books as *Cliff Castles and Cave Dwellings of Europe*, a volume so full of unusual information that any reader knowing nothing of its author might imagine that it was written by a single-minded enthusiast, describing a hobby that had filled every moment of his spare time for years, rather than the work of a professional journalist who could describe, with seemingly equal enthusiasm, almost anything from the proper use of the divining rod to the best way of building chimneys to prevent them from smoking. The mistake would be all the easier if the reader noticed that all the illustrations were reproductions of sketches made on the spot by Sabine himself.

Although he wrote over much, over quickly, and was at times unquestionably careless, and despite the fact that when dealing with subjects about which he felt deeply—and they were many—judicial impartiality was foreign to his nature, Sabine's work proves him to have been a born story-teller and writer; one to whom writing came as naturally as breathing.

Sixty-eight years after the publication of his first story, he received from his publisher, on the very day of his death, a copy of his last book.

12

The Eagle's Nest

Early Victorian England may seem a 'Green land far away' as the historian Arthur Bryant called it in *The English Saga*. But to us of the mid-twentieth century, even to those old enough to have personal memories of it, the England of before the first World War seems almost equally remote. The introduction of modern farm machinery, the passing of the carthorse, the coming of mains' water and electricity, the closing of many railways and the substitution of lorries, buses and cars, the widespread use of insecticides and weedkillers, have combined to change the pattern of life in farms and cottage almost beyond recognition. But though changed it still continues. That of the manor house, as Sabine knew it, has ceased to exist.

He was, as we have seen, a man who lived up to the limit of his income and was at times hard-pressed to make ends meet; but Lew House in the 1880s and 1890s housed his wife and himself, his enormous family, a governess, a dozen domestics and a fluctuating population of guests. Before his daughters married, even the long gallery upstairs, the pride of the house, had to be cut up into a number of small additional bedrooms. Over this huge household of more than thirty people, with outside staff of

The Eagle's Nest

a gardener, gardener's boy, groom and odd-job man, Grace ruled with quiet efficiency, though the task of caring for them must have presented innumerable problems, for Lew House stands more than nine miles away from the nearest market town and the village shop had of course none of those stocks of tinned and frozen foods that simplify catering today. Each day, staff and children were allotted their several tasks, and it was Grace and not Sabine who saw to it all. The estate and the parish were his concern, but once indoors there was nothing he desired except absolute punctuality at meals and an undisturbed library in which to write. The management of the house was her province. He was besides so frequently absent on his many quests that for years he lived in an intellectual dream-world and knew little about what went on in his own home. It was not till Grace became crippled and finally bed-ridden that Sabine had, as an old man, to try and cope with domestic problems, and his letters to Mary show how increasingly difficult he found the task. Until then it was Grace who saw to it all; Grace, who had started her working life as a child in clogs in the cotton mill at Horbury Brig. Yet today, while Sabine and his doings are still a living legend, she is almost forgotten even in Lew Trenchard. Arthur Baring-Gould's daughter, Mrs Irene Widdicombe, paid the following tribute to her memory:

Aunt Grace
Can personality ever change? I think not. It can be brought out and expanded, and that is all that happened to Aunt Grace. Her short education and her life with Uncle Sabine changed her manner of speech and no doubt enlarged her horizons, but I am convinced that the personality of Aunt Grace was the same which attracted Uncle Sabine to the beautiful mill girl. I am very sure that if she had not met him, but had married some humble labourer, she would have graced their cottage and brought up her family with the same dignity and the same pauky humour, and have been the same lovable person we knew at Lew House.

The Eagle's Nest

She was always the same whether entertaining at Lew House, being entertained in stately homes, chatting with farmers' wives, coping with her family and house, or sitting chatting in cottage kitchens. She never appeared ruffled however mad-cap her children were, however many people crowded into the house. Always the affectionate, happy smile, the rich and lovely talking voice.

The large staff she had to direct was not as excessive as one might think, for not only did the household have to depend on home-made jams and preserves, home-grown fruit and vegetables, home-cured bacon and hams and home-baked bread, all prepared by hand, but the housework had to be done without the aid of the simplest labour-saving devices. There was practically no plumbing of any sort and the water for bathing, washing and shaving had to be carried upstairs after being laboriously heated over the kitchen fire. The fireplaces were designed to burn logs which had to be sawn, split and carried in regularly. The only illumination was provided by candles and oil lamps, which meant that every candlestick had to be cleaned and every lamp filled and trimmed daily. Enormous quantities of food had to be prepared and cooked, for though wages were to our eyes infinitesimal, the servants' hall at 'the big house' always fed well and like the employers ate enormously by modern standards: the discipline of ration cards and two world wars was needed to change the eating habits of the English.

Meanwhile at Lew House the children were growing up under what would seem to us the strangest compound of over-strict discipline and almost unbelievable freedom. Punctually at eight o'clock each morning the house-bell rang and into the dining-room trooped the whole household for family prayers, the domestic staff primly perched on two rows of chairs, the family seated wherever there was space, occupying every niche and window-sill, for to be late for family prayers meant going without breakfast. The meal over and a second grace said, Sabine would

The Eagle's Nest

vanish to his library, the staff would go about their work and the children would be packed off to the schoolroom. Always meticulously punctual himself, Sabine would not tolerate unpunctuality in others, especially at mealtimes. To be even a few moments late would bring down a torrent of wrath upon the head of the offender, young or old.

Yet Sabine's children had long hours of completely unsupervised freedom; especially during the holidays, when the boys were home from school, the whole tribe ran wild when not actually under the eye of their parents. Was there a meet of the foxhounds in their vicinity, they would all be found at it, riding whatever mount was available. At times the Lew stables housed as many as a dozen horses and all would be pressed into service, riding horses, carriage horses, cart horses alike, even the little Dartmoor pony whose normal duty was to pull the lawn-mower. Their friends would sometimes lend them horses as well. It was said that there was nothing they could not ride, no hedge they would not jump. They grew to be considered indestructible. On one occasion Mary took a heavy toss and the MFH, seeing the fall, reined up and called anxiously: 'Who was that?' 'Mary Baring-Gould,' someone shouted back. 'That's all right then,' he said in a relieved voice. 'You can't kill one of that family.'

Before her marriage, Mary was known as a fine and fearless horsewoman. She loved the thrill of the cross-country gallop and the feel of a powerful horse under her, but she was exceptional in that even then she always had grave doubts about the ethics of hunting and in later life she would condemn the custom of 'blooding' a new recruit as frankly disgusting. None of her brothers and sisters seems to have shared Mary's doubts, and Sabine himself, though he took no interest in field sports, never objected to his sons and daughters riding to hounds. Sabine belonged to a generation that produced a number of foxhunting clergymen, among whom he counted several friends, and these he defended with his usual boldness, beginning his chapter on

The Eagle's Nest

'The Hunting Parson' in his book *Old Country Life*, with the words: 'Why not! Why should not the parson mount his cob and go after the hounds? . . . I had rather any day see a parson ride along with the pink, than sport the blue ribbon'. Needless to say this last remark brought a storm of protest from ardent total abstainers.

If Sabine was an old eagle, his children were certainly as wild as hawks, egging each other on. It was a fixed point of honour that all must follow where one led, girls and boys alike, and the piecemeal reconstruction of Lew House meant that there were usually ladders and scaffolding available on which the youngsters could indulge their taste for acrobatics. On one occasion two of them, Joan and John, were chasing their sister Cicely along the planks above the ballroom, when suddenly she missed her footing and vanished. She was still unconscious when the workmen engaged on the building picked her up and carried her indoors. Her brother and sister, believing her dead, hid themselves in panic, but in later life they denied the story, since widely told, that they attempted to bury her for fear of what their father might say.

But their most dangerous games centred round the lake-quarry. The boat-house, their headquarters, consisted of one large room overlooking the lake, with the boat stored beneath it. In this they spent much of their time, free from parental authority, picnicking and sometimes even sleeping there. The one leaky boat was far too small to take them all, so all sorts of additional craft were called into service whenever they felt the urge to seek adventure on the 40-ft. deep waters. These varied from home-made rafts to worn-out hip-baths, discarded from domestic use and patched with wood and bottle corks. In these they paddled about the lake, crossing to the waterfall and holding impromptu water tournaments that often ended in a spill. Mary, who for some reason or other never learnt to swim, was almost drowned during one of these frolics, but the family luck

The Eagle's Nest

held and she was dragged ashore, unconscious but still alive. A large fire was immediately kindled on the shore near the boathouse. Her clothes were dried, she recovered consciousness, to the relief of her brothers and sisters, and most important of all in their eyes, their parents never learnt of the incident.

The boys would sometimes spend the whole night poaching pheasants in Lew Wood, in company with the village poacher, for the sporting rights of the estate were let to Mr Sperling and carefully preserved.

The younger generation at Lew House formed a closely knit and self-contained unit, a tribe which neither needed nor encouraged outside contacts, though they were sociable enough in their own way. Neighbouring families were apt to eye them askance, though the beauty and vivacity of the girls drew young men to Lew from miles around. It took considerable courage to come courting a Miss Baring-Gould, for suitors were subjected to a great deal of chaff and innumerable practical jokes, not only from Sabine's children but, most unexpectedly to those who did not know him intimately, from Sabine himself. His favourite toy was a 'plate-lifter', two rubber bulbs joined by a rubber tube. One bulb was placed under the tablecloth beneath a guest's plate and while he talked Sabine would gently squeeze the other, rocking the plate. He would use it especially on any guest whom he suspected of indulging in a glass too many, and so skilfully did he manipulate it that on one occasion at least the unfortunate visitor uttered a muttered word of apology and rushed headlong from the room. Sabine retained this curious form of humour throughout his life and during the first World War he went to considerable trouble to fake 'call-up' papers for his stepmother's fat and aged pony, and sent them to Ardoch Lodge in a buff OHMS envelope, greatly to the old lady's consternation.

Harvey Dickinson, as the first to come wooing a Miss Baring-Gould, bore the full brunt of the family's sense of humour, his

The Eagle's Nest

bald head—for though he lived to be over ninety he was bald from youth—making him a particularly easy target. He married Mary Baring-Gould on 11 January 1893. Sabine officiated himself and the marriage of his eldest daughter moved him so deeply that for once the letter that he wrote to her during the following week was not only intimate and personal but very emotional. He still retained his ironic humour, however, when describing the tenants' dinner which followed the wedding:

> All however has gone well. The farmers and their wives were very happy on Thursday. Mr. —— said to Julian 'If-if-if- jush one more sup of grog—we'd ha-ha-ha-have been puffectly happy.' But they had had quite enough. They sat from 1-4.30 over their dishes and grog. Mr. —— proposed your health and his eyes filled with tears when he spoke of you and I believe most of the company, and this was before the grog came on, were moved. Afterwards one could have understood it. . . .'

The letter goes on to ask Mary to find time even on her honeymoon to write a soothing letter to one couple who were deeply hurt because she had not personally asked them to the festivities and who would otherwise probably show their indignation by never coming to church again.

However reckless and unconventional, not one of the Baring-Goulds was either lazy or stupid and they all had the gift of making the most of their opportunities. Mary, for example, never had any schooling except for the short time she spent with the nuns in Germany. Her only other teacher was the formidable Miss Biggs, though her father supervised her reading, and books played almost as great a part in her life as they did in his.

Sabine had small opinion of the modern novels of his day, including his own, and did not consider them suitable reading for the young. The sickly-sweet stories then written for children revolted him. One in particular, called *Ministering Children*, he particularly disliked and any copy of it, presented at Christ-

The Eagle's Nest

mas by misguided relatives, always vanished, for fear it might turn his children into pious little prigs. The stiff reading that Sabine advised might well have discouraged a less ardent reader, but Mary loved books. In consequence by the time of her marriage, she had read most of Shakespeare, Scott, Dickens and Thackeray and had absorbed the standard historians from Gibbon to Macaulay. Sabine even encouraged her to read Fielding in order to learn something of what human nature was really like. She had the mind of a librarian and could tell you instantly the name of the author of any book she had ever read. She was also a skilled and ardent gardener with a practical knowledge of flower growing, and an expert needlewoman, though she lacked the artistic flair possessed by her sister Margaret, whose home-made dresses were of such a high standard that as an art student in London she was seriously asked how she could possibly afford to wear Paris frocks.

Theirs was a world far removed from our own. The whole family, to a greater or less degree, inherited or acquired Sabine's own disregard for outside opinion. To their acquaintances they always remained something of an enigma, but to those in trouble the help they gave was not so much an unavoidable obligation as a natural reaction like eating or sleeping.

It is unfortunate that during these years no visitors' book seems to have been kept, and as the memory of ageing persons is not a reliable guide there is no record of the numerous people who enjoyed the hospitality of Lew House, but they were an interesting set to meet, for the one thing Sabine could not tolerate was stupidity. Cecil Sharp was at one time, as we have seen, a regular visitor, and one might any time encounter a foreign professor or man of letters with whom Sabine had become friendly on his travels. The one person reasonably certain not to be met at Lew was a Church dignitary; the dislike was mutual. Several distinguished archaeologists made Lew House their headquarters when visiting Devon, among them the Rev W. C. Lukis, an

The Eagle's Nest

authority on the prehistoric alignments on Dartmoor, which he measured and mapped for the Royal Society of Antiquaries. Sabine refers to him in a paper that he contributed to the *Transactions* of the Devonshire Association, describing a monolith that he discovered while repairing Lew Mill. This had for long been used to span the mill-leat and when he discovered what it was, Sabine had it cleaned and erected in front of the mill, where it still stands; another memorial to the trouble he took to preserve the monuments of the past.

13

'Now the Day is Over'

In August 1914, when the first World War broke out, Sabine was in his eightieth year. Had he died then, his life would have been complete. For his age he was still active and mentally alert. For thirty years he had been the kindly if autocratic monarch of his own small world in Lew Trenchard. He had seen the fulfilment of most of his life's ambitions and had made for himself an honoured name in the world of letters. Yet so great was his vitality that he was to linger on like some sad ghost from another world for ten more years, for him increasingly unhappy ones.

None of the many wars that had occurred during his lifetime had apparently influenced or even greatly interested him. He had disapproved of the Boer War in principle, but this disapproval had been more political than personal. To him, as to many nineteenth-century Englishmen, the word 'war' implied little more than the periodic frontier struggles of an expanding Empire; something which one could take pride in or disapprove of, according to one's outlook and upbringing, but which was primarily a matter for professional soldiers. Foreigners might possibly suffer the miseries of war and the horrors of invasion, but not the English; their Navy had for a century ensured their immunity. To us, the weary survivors of two world wars, living permanently beneath the shadow of yet more terrible possibilities, it is an outlook hard to understand and harder still to excuse.

Not till he was old did Sabine for the first time realise something of the tragic meaning of war. Not only were sons and grandsons of his own serving in the armed forces, and the young men of his parish, whom he had known and loved from childhood, leaving never to return, but the old Europe, the heart of the civilisation to which he belonged, was disintegrating before his eyes. With his love of Europe and his many friends in Germany, France, Italy and Belgium, the struggle had for him something of the added horror of civil war. Desperately he tried to shut his mind to it and to continue writing of what he knew and understood, but the things that interested him and of which he was competent to write, no longer had any appeal for a people engaged in a life-and-death struggle.

He had written no fiction for the past ten years and now he had the humiliation of knowing that, for the time at least, he had lost his reading public altogether. From the publication of *The Church Revival* in 1914 until 1920, when its sequel *The Evangelical Revival* appeared, nothing that he wrote found a publisher.

Grace was by this time almost completely crippled by a painful illness and required attention day and night. Trained nurses were unobtainable in wartime, and to add to his difficulties Sabine again found himself hard-pressed for money. On 27 January 1915 he wrote despairingly to Mary: 'With income tax at 7/6 in the pound, I have made up my mind that at Michaelmas I will move with Mamma into a small lodging at Plymouth. I cannot possibly keep this house going.'

But he never did so, for when the time came Grace was too ill to be moved. In the following year she died, and after that nothing really seemed worth the effort. Almost overnight he became a very old man. On her tombstone in Lew Trenchard

'Now the Day is Over'

churchyard he caused to be inscribed the words.

DIMIDIUM ANIMAE MEAE ('half my life')

And it was true. Not only had she borne his many children and skilfully directed his complex household, she had been his constant and wise companion, whose shrewd advice had saved him repeatedly from many quarrels and mistakes, and above all she had given him what to a man of his nature mattered most of all: a feeling of deep security and peace.

He had been the builder, but it was she who had turned his dream-building into a home. Now deprived of the solace of her presence, his powers of body and mind at last began to fail him. He no longer spent hours standing at the high desk in his library but sat beside the fire in his bedroom composing his reminiscences. These were planned to appear in three volumes, the first of which, *Early Reminiscences,* was published in 1923 and the second, *Further Reminiscences* in 1925, the year after his death. Of the third volume no trace can now be found, though he certainly wrote at least part of it and had been planning it as early as 1920, for in that year he commissioned an illustration for it from his eldest grandson, Arscott Dickinson, and in a letter dated 23 July 1920, he sent Mary exact instructions of what he required; the costumes worn by the parson of the Hanoverian period, the Tractarian parson, the Evangelical parson, the High Church parson and, finally, he demanded, with a flash of his old irony, a picture of the modern curate, 'who has shed his tail like a tadpole transformed into a frog and who exposes his hindquarters to the admiration of the faithful.'

In October of the same year he wrote another letter, expressing his delight at receiving the drawing (reproduced on page 72) and mentioning that he did not intend the third volume of his reminiscences to be published until fifteen years after his death. Today, all that can be traced of the manuscript is the illustration in question, which was found among Mary's papers. Not only the

'Now the Day is Over'

whole of the third volume of reminiscences has vanished, but a chapter on his marriage with Grace was cut out of the second volume. That he wrote it is certain, for another letter to Mary, written on 13 September 1923, mentions that he is enclosing a copy of it for her to read through and comment upon.

As increasing infirmity confined him more and more to his room, Sabine began at last to lose touch even with his own little world, and was forced to leave the care of the parish almost entirely to his curate, Gilbert Arundell. He was growing feeble, and it is unfortunate that by far the finest portrait of him was not painted until four years before his death, when some at least of the power and vitality that was his most outstanding characteristic had already left his face. In 1920 he was persuaded by his relatives to sit for his portrait and Melton Fisher, RA was commissioned to paint it. It is a splendid picture (page 17), but Sabine viewed it with mixed feelings, describing it in a letter to Mary as 'a picture of an old decrepit boat'.

These were sad and lonely years for the old man and far from easy ones for those who cared for him, for towards the end he became querulous and at times unreasonable. Mary was able to come over frequently from her home at Dunsland, and during the hours that she sat alone with him in his room she probably heard a number of complaints, for he had begun to resent, with the feeble anger of old age, the fact that he was no longer the unquestioned autocrat in his own house; but Mary had the gift of silence and never disclosed their conversations.

Three personal memories of Sabine in his last years come fleetingly to mind. The first is of a visit that he paid to Dunsland only a year or two before his death with the express purpose of seeing once more the house from which he had copied so much when reconstructing Lew House, and which he had used as an illustration in his book *An Old English Home*. The second memory is of him standing bare-headed and robed as he dedicated the war memorial on Lewdown commemorating the men

'Now the Day is Over'

who served and died in the war that shattered his world. The third is of a very different scene. Perhaps it is the 'coming out' party of his grand-daughter Adèle Baring-Gould, for a dance is taking place in the ballroom and the house is for the last time filled to overflowing with his children and grandchildren. Across the years that intervene one hears the music and laughter—and then there is a hush. Standing in the doorway, clad in the black-velvet evening suit that he affected, and leaning heavily on two sticks, is the owner and builder of it all. For the first time in the eyes of those present he no longer looks dominating and impressive, only a very tired, feeble old man. Mary is at his side in a moment, guiding his stumbling feet and helping him to a chair. The music rises; laughter fills the room again.

His end, when at last it came, was quite peaceful and the Church of England which he had loved, served and continually offended by his outspokenness, and which had in consequence so long and steadfastly refused to recognise his services in any way, did him some belated honour at last. The long procession of robed clergy, which included, in addition to those of the Deanery of Tavistock, his half-brother Arthur, his curate Gilbert Arundell and one of his former curates, the Rev K. A. Lake, vicar of Heavitree, stretched from the gates of his home to the gates of his church, both of which he had designed. Two bishops, Lord William Cecil of Exeter and Dr J. H. B. Masterman of Plymouth, shared the service and a number of minor Church dignitaries were present as well. The coffin was carried on the old parish hand-bier by tenants of the Lew Trenchard estate.

Many of Sabine's children followed the coffin with their families including Mary (Mrs Dickinson), Margaret (Mrs Rowe), Veronica (Mrs King), Barbara (Mrs Burnard), Joan (Mrs Priestley), and Grace (Mrs Calmady-Hamlyn), and of the crowd that followed them not one-third could find standing room in the church. The reporters hovered round and cameras clicked: for the last time Sabine Baring-Gould was in the news.

'Now the Day is Over'

During the service they sang the hymns that he had written so long before; 'Onward, Christian Soldiers', to which the children of his mission had marched at Horbury Brig; 'On the Resurrection Morning', in which Queen Victoria is said to have found comfort when she lost her husband; 'Through the Night of Doubt and Sorrow'; and at the graveside where they laid him beside Grace they sang his children's hymn, 'Now the Day is Over'.

His day was indeed over; he had outlived it by a decade. The old social order into which he had been born was rapidly disintegrating, its decay greatly accelerated by the war. Outwardly at least all that seemed left was on the one hand the flaunting, money-mad vulgarity of the war profiteers and on the other hand the bitter disillusionment of the ex-servicemen, who had returned to nothing but mass unemployment, the means test and the dole. The old estates were breaking up, the manor closing. Traditional values were in the melting pot. The very things to which Sabine had dedicated his life and for which he had fought so hard had become objects of mistrust and ridicule. It was indeed time for him to be gone from a world that no longer held in reverence the things that he knew and loved.

Yet his hymns are still sung a century after they were written; some at least of his books are still read; the houses that he designed and built are still occupied; the ancient monuments that he helped to preserve are now safe from vandals and souvenir hunters, protected by the State; the traditional songs that he saved from oblivion have become a national heritage. The little church, the lantern that he prepared for the Christ he served, still dreams gently on, half-hidden today by the woods that enclose the churchyard in which he lies at rest beside his wife, surrounded by members of his family and his parishioners.

Here we can pause and feel for a nostalgic moment something of that older, fast-vanishing England in which he lived and of which he loved to write.

The Works of Sabine

FICTION

The Chorister. A Tale of King's College Chapel during the Civil War	1856
Through Flood and Flame (3 vols)	1868
In Exitu Israel (2 vols)	1870
Ernestine (a translation from the German)	1879
Mehalah (2 vols)	1880
John Herring (3 vols)	1883
Court Royal (3 vols)	1886
Golden Feather (SPCK Penny Library of Fiction)	1886
The Gaverocks (3 vols)	1887
Red Spider (2 vols)	1887
Little Tu'penny (in parts)	1887-1903
Richard Cable, the Lighterman (3 vols)	1888
Eve (2 vols)	1888
The Pennycomequicks (3 vols)	1889
Arminell (3 vols)	1890
Grettir the Outlaw (free translation of *The Saga of Grettir the Strong*)	1890
My Prague Pig and Other Stories (for children)	1890
Jacquetta and Other Stories	1890
Margery of Quether and Other Stories	1891
Urith (3 vols)	1891
Fifteen Pounds (SPCK Penny Library of Fiction)	1891

Bibliography

In the Roar of the Sea (3 vols)	1892
Through all the Changing Scenes of Life	1892
Mrs Curgenven of Curgenven (3 vols)	1893
Cheap Jack Zita (3 vols)	1893
The Two Brents (SPCK Penny Library of Fiction)	1893
The Icelander's Sword	1894
The Queen of Love (3 vols)	1894
Kitty Alone (3 vols)	1895
Naomi	1895
The Broom-Squire	1896
Dartmoor Idylls (short stories)	1896
Guavas the Tinner	1897
Bladys of the Stewponey	1897
Perpetua	1897
Domitia	1898
In a Quiet Village	1898
Furze Bloom (short stories)	1899
Pabo the Priest	1899
Winifred	1900
Royal Georgie	1901
The Frobishers (first published as a serial in *The Queen* under the title *Our Joan*)	1901
Miss Quillet	1902
Nebo the Nailer	1902
Chris of All-sorts	1903
In Dewisland	1904
Siegfried	1904
Sedlescombe Fogue (*Daily Mail Penny Stories*)	1904
Monsieur Fichelmere and Other Stories	1905

Short Stories in Other Books and Periodicals

Gottlieb's Picture (in *Please tell me a Tale*)	1885
My Prague Pig (in *My Birthday Present*)	1886
Wow-wow (in *Just One More Tale*)	1886

Bibliography

The Queen of Dentists (in *Just One More Tale*)	1886
The Cat's Tree (in *Jack Frost's Little Prisoners*)	1887
The Schnabelweild Plot (in *Jack Frost's Little Prisoners*)	1897
The New Master (in *Stories Jolly, Stories New*)	1889
Master Sacristan Eberhardt (1858?)	
The Dead Trumpeter (1860?) (Reprinted in	
The Fireman (1860?) *Hurst's Echoes*)	1890
Daddy Treellis (in *Under One Cover*, a volume of stories by various authors)	1898

OPERA

Red Spider (libretto and lyrics for operatic version) 1897

RELIGIOUS WORKS

1 *Hymns, poems, songs, etc*

On the Resurrection Morning (written in 1863 at the time of his mother's death)	*Church Times*	1864
Onward, Christian Soldiers	*Church Times*	1864
Now the Day is Over	*Church Times*	1867
Through the Night of Doubt and Sorrow (translated from the Danish and first published in *The People's Hymnal*		1867(?)
Church Songs (2 vols. Words and music)		1884
Church Songs (words only. For use in Lew Trenchard Church)	vol 1	1911
	vol 2	1912
Easter Eve. A Poem (1860). Published in *Hurst's Echoes*		1890

2 *Essays*

The Revival of Religious Confraternities
  (in *The Church and the World*, 1st series)   1865

Bibliography

Origins of the Schools of Thought in the English Church (in *The Church and the World*, 3rd series)	1868

3 *Tracts and pamphlets*

Caught Napping	1866
Only a Ghost	1870
Luther and Justification	1871
Protestant or Catholic?	1872
Short Answers to Objections about Religion	1874
Popular Objections to a Mission Answered	1874
Wafted Away	1876
Evening Communion	1895
The Present Crisis	1899
The Church of England and its Irreconcilables	1900

4 *Sermons*

One Hundred Sermon Sketches for Extempore Preachers	1871
Village Preaching for a Year, 1st Series (2 vols)	1875
Twenty Sermon Sketches (in a supplement to vol 2 of *Village Preaching* in 2nd and subsequent editions)	1876
Sermons to Children, 1st Series (2 vols)	1879
The Preacher's Pocket	1880
Village Preaching for Saints' Days	1881
Village Preaching for a Year, 2nd Series (2 vols)	1884
Sermons for Children, 2nd Series	1907
Village Sermons for Simple Souls	1912
My Last Few Words	1924

5 *Single sermons* (printed in pamphlet form)

Organisation (preached at St Michael's, Wakefield)	1870
Secular versus Religious Education (preached at St Peter's, London Docks)	1872

Bibliography

The Power of the Press (preached at St Paul's, Walworth)	1873

6 *Sermons in collections by various authors*

Thanksgiving (in *Plain Preaching for Poor People*)	1872
Bad Example (in *Plain Preaching for Poor People*)	1873
A Time of Love (in *Plain Preaching for Poor People*)	1874
The Future of Creation (in *Plain Preaching for a Year*, Series 1)	1872
The Lord hath need of Him (in *Plain Preaching for a Year*, Series 1)	1873
Unmoveable in Christ (in *Plain Preaching for a Year*, Series 1)	1873
Humiliation a Sign of Conversion (in *Plain Preaching for a Year*, Series 1)	1873
Our Heavenly Home (in *Plain Preaching for a Year*, Series 1)	1873
The Sight of God (in *Plain Preaching for a Year*, Series 1)	1873
Vigilance (in *Plain Preaching for a Year*, Series 1)	1873
The Well of Grace (in *The Catholic Pulpit*)	1876
Simplicity (in *Plain Preaching for a Year*, Series 2)	1876
The Epiphany (in *Plain Preaching for a Year*, Series 3)	1881
Christ standing in the Midst (in *Plain Preaching for a Year*, Series 3)	1882
Plain Duties (in *Plain Preaching for a Year*, Series 3)	1882
Motives (in *Plain Preaching for a Year*, Series 3)	1882
The Spirit of Love (in *The Literary Churchman Series*)	1880
Christmas. A Pattern for Worship (in *The Literary Churchman Series*)	1883
Think on Me (in *The Literary Churchman Series*)	1884
Sowing and Reaping (in *Harvest Preaching*, 1st Series)	1885
Patience (in *Kindly Fruits of the Earth*)	1889
From Above (in *Sermons for the Coronation of Edward VII*)	1902
Sunday (in *Sermons on Sunday Observance*)	1907

Bibliography

The Coronation (one of two sermons for the Coronation of George V) 1911

7 Books

Post-Medieval Preachers	1865
The Path of the Just. Tales of Holy Men and Children	1867
The Origin and Development of Religious Belief (2 vols)	1869-1870
The Golden Gate. A Manual of Devotions. 3 parts,	1869-1870
new edition	1896
The Legendary Lives of Old Testament Characters (2 vols)	1872
The Lives of the Saints. 15-volume edition	1872-1877
16-volume edition	1897-1898
new 16-volume edition	1914
Village Conferences on the Creed	1873
The Lost and Hostile Gospels	1874
Some Modern Difficulties	1875
The Mystery of Suffering	1877
The Seven Last Words	1884
The Passion of Jesus	1885
Our Parish Church	1885
The Birth of Jesus	1885
Nazareth and Capernaum	1886
The Trial of Jesus	1886
The Way of Sorrows	1887
The Death and Resurrection of Jesus	1888
Our Inheritance	1888
Conscience and Sin	1890
The Church in Germany	1891
A Study of St Paul	1897
The Sunday Round (2 vols)	1900
Virgin Saints and Martyrs	1907
The Restitution of All Things	1907

Bibliography

St Francis de Sales (selections from)	1907
Lives of the British Saints (4 vols. With John Fisher DD)	1907-1913
The Church Revival	1914
The Evangelical Revival	1920

BIOGRAPHIES

The Vicar of Morwenstowe	1876
The Tragedy of the Caesars (2 vols)	1892
1-volume edition	1895
The Life of Napoleon Bonaparte	1897
abridged edition	1908
A Memorial of Horatio Nelson	1905
Nero (Royal Library. Belles Lettres Series)	1907

FOLK SONGS

The Songs of the West (first published in 4 parts)	1889-1891
1-volume edition	1892
Cecil Sharp edition (revised)	1905
A Garland of Country Song	1895
English Minstrelsie (8 vols)	1895-1897
English Folk Songs for Schools (with Cecil Sharp)	1906

MYTH, FOLK-LORE AND FAIRY STORIES

The Book of Were-wolves	1865
Household Tales (appendix to Henderson's *Folk Lore of the Northern Counties*)	1866
Curious Myths of the Middle Ages, 1st series	1866
Curious Myths of the Middle Ages, 2nd series	1868
A Book of Fairy Tales, retold	1894

Bibliography

Introduction to *Fairy Tales from Grimm*	1894
Old English Fairy Tales	1895
The Crock of Gold (fairy tales)	1899
A Book of Ghosts	1904
A Book of Folk-Lore	1913

GUIDE BOOKS AND BOOKS ON TRAVEL

Iceland, its Scenes and Sagas	1863
Germany, Past and Present (2 vols)	1879
abridged edition	1881
Germany (*Foreign Countries and British Colonies*)	1883
Germany (with A. Gilman) written for *The Story of the Nations* Series	1886
In Troubadour Land	1891
The Deserts of Southern France (2 vols)	1894
A Book of the West, Volume 1 : Devon	1899
A Book of the West, Volume 2 : Cornwall	1899
A Book of Dartmoor	1900
A Book of Brittany	1901
Brittany (*Methuen's Little Guides*)	1902
A Book of North Wales	1903
A Book of South Wales	1905
A Book of the Riviera	1905
A Book of the Rhine	1906
A Book of the Pyrenees	1907
Devon (*Methuen's Little Guides*)	1907
A Book of the Cevennes	1907
Cornwall (*Cambridge County Geographies*)	1910
Cliff Castles and Cave Dwellings in Europe	1911
The Land of Teck and its Neighbours	1911
Sheepstor (pamphlet)	1912
Shaw Prior (pamphlet)	1914
Lew Trenchard Church (unsigned)	1915

Bibliography

GENERAL

The Silver Store (poems collected from medieval, Christian and Jewish mines)	1868
Curiosities of Olden Times	1869
revised edition	1895
Yorkshire Oddities and Strange Events (2 vols)	1874
Historical Oddities and Strange Events, Series 1	1889
Historical Oddities and Strange Events, Series 2	1891
Freaks of Fanaticism	1893
Old Country Life (ran to four editions by 1892)	1889
Strange Survivals	1892
A Book of Nursery Songs and Rhymes	1895
An Armoury of the Western Counties (with R. Twigge)	1898
An Old English Home	1898
A Coronation Souvenir (Edward VII)	1912
Amazing Adventures (A Children's Picture Book)	1903
Devonshire Characters and Strange Events (2 vols)	1908
Cornish Characters and Strange Events (2 vols)	1909
History of Sarawak under its White Rajahs (with C. A. Bamfylde)	1909
Family Names and their History	1910
Coronation Souvenir (George V)	1911
Early Reminiscences (1834-1864)	1923
Further Reminiscences (1864-1894), published posthumously	1925

GENERAL PAMPHLETS AND ESSAYS

How to save Fuel	1874
Wagner's Parzival at Bayreuth	1892
Colour in Composition (*On the Art of Writing Fiction*)	1894
James Lawless, Innkeeper (50 copies only)	1907

Bibliography

Addenda

Early Pedigree of the Baring Family (almost certainly only intended for private circulation)	undated
The Baring-Gould Selection Reader (H. G. Rose)	1906
The Baring-Gould Continuous Reader (H. G. Rose)	1908
Thoughts from Baring-Gould (H. B. Elliot)	1916
The Ancient Settlements on Trewortha Marsh (*Journal* of the Royal Institution of Cornwall)	1892
Further Account of the Ancient Settlements on Trewortha Marsh (*Journal* of the Royal Institution of Cornwall)	1893
The Early History of Cornwall (Presidential Address) (*Journal* of the Royal Institution of Cornwall)	1898
The Early Celtic Saints (Presidential Address) (*Journal* of the Royal Institution of Cornwall)	1899
A large number of contributions, ranging from folk-lore, dialect and customs to archaeology, to the *Transactions* of the Devonshire Association	1878-1896
Prehistoric Remains on Dartmoor (Presidential Address) (*Transactions* of the Devonshire Association)	1896

Author's Note

Even this list is almost certainly incomplete. Many pamphlets, articles and short stories in long-forgotten journals must be still untraced.

In compiling this bibliography I owe a great debt to the memory of the late Rev F. G. S. Nicholle, who was a life-long admirer and collector of Sabine Baring-Gould's writings.

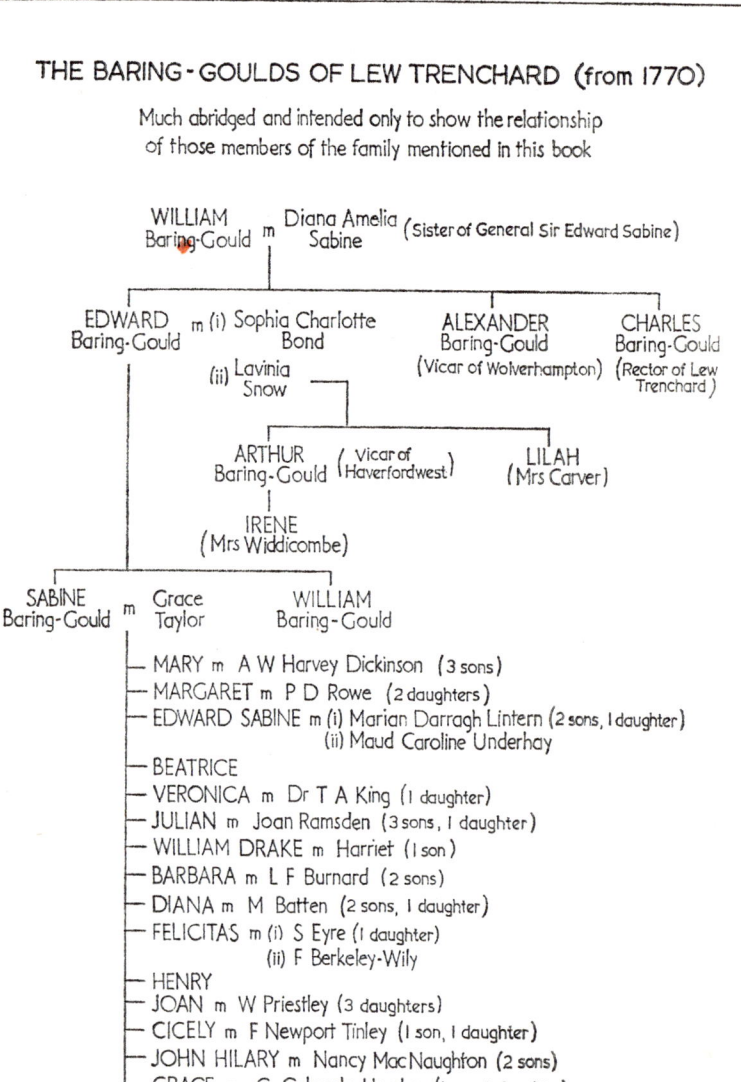

Index

Anderson, Rev J. K., 159
Ardoch Lodge, 78, 80, 166
Arminell, 105
Arscott of Tetcott, (folk-song), 125
Arundell, Rev Gilbert 79, 113, 173, 174

Backward Christian Soldiers (D. Dewar), 50
Baldersby, 51
Baring, Charles, 15
Baring-Gould, Adèle (granddaughter), 174
Baring-Gould, Rev Alexander (uncle), 15, 28, 94
Baring-Gould, Rev Arthur (half-brother), 12, 62, 64, 78, 94, 95, 174
Baring-Gould, Beatrice (daughter), 63
Baring-Gould, Rev Charles (uncle), 15, 22, 62, 66, 74, 78, 118
Baring-Gould, Charlotte, née Bond (mother), 16, 20, 28, 42
Baring-Gould, Edward (father), 15, 16, 21, 26, 28, 34, 40, 42, 61, 62, 106, 113
Baring-Gould, Edward (son), 58, 63, 69, 87
Baring-Gould, Grace (wife), 55-8, 69, 84, 108, 112, 162, 171
Baring-Gould, Henry (son), 64, 87, 88
Baring-Gould, John (son), 64, 89, 165

Baring-Gould, Julian (son), 63, 88
Baring-Gould, Lavinia, née Snow (step-mother), 78
Baring-Gould, Marion (daughter-in-law), 88
Baring-Gould, William (grandfather), 15, 22
Baring-Gould, William (brother), 62
Baring-Gould, William (son), 63, 88
Baring-Gould, William Stuart (grandson), 88
Barrie, Sir J. M., 101, 143
Batten, Diana Amelia (daughter), 63
Berkely-Wiley, Felicitas (daughter), 63, 111
Betjeman, John, 68
Bickersteth, E. H. (Bishop of Exeter), 47
Bickersteth, Robert (Bishop of Ripon), 43
Biggs, Miss, 73, 87, 167
Black Forest, 69, 70, 157
Bolitho, T. R., 158
Bond, Frederick (uncle), 32
Book of Brittany, A, 154
Book of the Cevennes, A, 154
Book of Dartmoor, A, 157
Book of North Wales, A, 155
Book of the Pyrenees, A, 154
Book of the Rhine, A, 154
Book of the Riviera, A, 154
Book of South Wales, A, 155
Book of the West, A, 119, 155, 156

Index

Borders of Tamar and Tavy (Bray), 25
Bouché, Carl de, 121
Branscombe, Mr, 120
Bratton Clovelly, 15, 144
Bray, Rev Edward Atkyns, 25
Brierly, Samuel, 29
British Museum Library, 134
Brittany, 154
Broadbury Gibbet (song), 138
Broadley Chapel, 98
Brooke, Rajah, 88
Broom Squire, The, 144
Bryant, Arthur, 161
Burnard, Robert, 25, 141, 159
Burnard, Barbara (daughter), 63, 174
Burns, Robert, 134
Bussell, Dr F. W., 128, 129, 141
Butt, Clara, 111

Calmady-Hamlyn, Grace (daughter), 64, 174
Cambridge, 28-31
Carver, Lilah (half-sister), 62, 64, 78
Cecil, Lord William (Bishop of Exeter), 174
Chartists, 13
Chorister, The, 30
Church Times, The, 46, 47, 50
Church Revival, The, 33, 148, 149, 171
Churchill, Winston, 47
Cliff Castles and Cave Dwellings in Europe, 160
Condy (artist), 119
Coombe Trenchard, 80
Cornish Characters and Strange Events, 151
Cornish moors, 81, 102
Curiosities of Olden Times, 151
Curious Myths of the Middle Ages, 24, 150

Dakers, Lionel, 49
Dalton, 51-60, 92, 142
Dartmoor, 24, 31, 81, 102, 104, 142, 143, 156, 157, 169
— Exploration Committee, 31, 158
Dartmoor Idylls, 157
Davey, Charles, 123
Deserts of Southern France, The, 154
Deschwanden, Paul, 121
Devonshire Association, The, 139, 158, 169
Devonshire Characters and Strange Events, 151
Dickinson, Arscott, S. H. (grandson), 12, 89, 121, 172
Dickinson, A. W. Harvey (son-in-law), 59, 78, 96, 107, 108, 166
Dickinson, Mary (daughter), 11, 48, 56, 58, 63, 69, 70, 73, 78, 83-7, 96, 98, 101 106, 108, 111, 112, 114, 129, 135, 144-6, 154, 155, 164, 165, 167, 171, 173, 174
The Dilly Song (folk song) 136
Doidge, F. C., 77
Downe, Viscountess, 51, 55
Doyle, Sir Arthur Conan, 55
Drysdale, Learmont, 145
Dunsland House, 108, 129, 173
Dustan, Charles, 83, 84

East Mersea, 61-74, 92, 142
The English Church and Nation (Maldon) 33
Encyclopaedia Britannica, 142
The English Parson (W. Addison) 11
English Folk-songs for Schools, 137
Enys, J. D., 159
Episcopal 'Black Book', 90
Ernestine, 64
Evangelical Revival, The 148, 149, 171

Fisher, Melton, RA, 173
Folk Songs of Somerset (Cecil Sharp), 136
Fone, Samuel, 130
Footsteps of Former Men in Cornwall (R. S. Hawker), 150, 151
Freiburg, 69

Index

Frobishers, The, 155

Gatrill, Rev, J. M., 66, 69, 113
Galleford, Battle of, 159
Germany, 153
Germany, Past and Present, 153
Gladstone, W. E., 60
Gold, John, 14
Goodwin, Rev Harvey, 26
Gould, Captain Edward, 14
Gould, Henry, 14
Gould, James, 14
Gould, Margaret, 15
Gould, 'Old Madam', 15
Gould, Col William, 14
Great Exhibition, The, 21
Great Welsh Churchmen and their Prayers, 78
Grettir the Outlaw, 38, 39, 133, 144
Gurney, Sir Goldsworthy, 151

Hardy, Thomas, 144
Harmsworth, H. C., 49
Harmsworth, Sir Leicester, 48
Hawker, Rev R. S., 149, 151
Hay, Ian, 49
Henwood Gold Medal, 159
Herbert, George, 76
Historical Oddities and Strange Events, 151
History, Gazetteer and Directory of Devon (White), 92
Hockin, J., 134
Holy Club, The, 29, 42, 64
Horbury Brig, 43, 44, 45, 46, 52, 130
Huggins, William, 127, 138
Humperdinck, Engelbert, 145
Hurstpierpoint School, 37, 43, 91
Huxley, Professor, 60

Iceland, 39
Iceland. Its Scenes and Sagas, 40, 153
In Exitu Israel, 64
In the Roar of the Sea, 144
In Troubadour Land, 154

Keble, Rev John, 37

King, Veronica (daughter), 63, 69, 174
King's College School, 19
Kingsley, Rev Charles, 31, 37
Knowles, Mr, 46

Lancing School, 37
Land of Teck and its Neighbours, The, 154
Last of the Singers, The (song), 139
Lavidière (painter), 56, 121
Lake, Rev, K. E., 174
Laycock, C. H., 139
Lewis, C. S., 149
Lives of the Saints, 65, 66, 148
Lowe, Dr, 38
Lowder, Rev, Charles Fuge, 33
Lukis, Rev W. C., 168
Luxton, Roger, 126

Maid of Sker, The (Blackmore), 79
Mansfield, Mr, 115
Marlborough Grammar School, 32
Malines, St Jacques church, 121
Masterman, Dr (Bishop of Plymouth), 174
Mehalah, 40, 64, 65, 66, 144
Maurois, André, 21
Metternich, Prince, 16
Ministering Children, 167
Miss Quillet, 155
Mole Catcher, The (folk-song), 134
Monk, Sir Thomas, 14

Nebo the Nailer, 155
New Statesman, The, 144
Newton St Petrock, 118
Northey, Mrs, 12
Now the Day is Over (hymn), 48, 175

Old Country Life, 79, 107, 110, 126, 139, 152, 165
Old English Home, An, 107, 152, 173
On the Resurrection Morning (hymn), 46, 48, 175
Onward, Christian Soldier (W. Purcell), 11, 47, 98, 100

Index

Onward Christian Soldiers (hymn), 46-50, 175
Orchard Farm, 107
Ordination, 43
Origin and Development of Religious Belief, The, 59, 148
Oxford Companion to Music, The, 136
Oxford Dictionary of the Christian Church, The, 29

Pabo the Priest, 144
Padstowe, 118
Parry, Sir James, 34
Parsons, James (the Singing Machine), 127
Pau, 23, 24
Pengelly (coachman), 16
Pepys, Samuel, 110
Perambulations of Dartmoor (Rowe), 25
Petrock, St, 118, 119
Petrockstowe, 118
Pinwell, the Misses, 119, 120
Plymouth City Library, 133
Priestley, Joan (daughter), 12, 64, 94, 99, 137, 157, 165, 174
Prince Consort, 19
Purcell, William, 11, 47, 68, 98, 100

Quest of the Sangraal, The (Hawker), 150

Radford, Daniel, 124
Ramps, The (Rampenstein), 113, 128
Red Spider, 144-7
Reform Bill, The, 32
Reminiscences, 16, 24, 25, 28, 33, 37, 39, 47, 52, 55, 66, 69, 73, 93, 94, 105, 123, 172
Rise of the Dutch Republic (Motley), 58
Roberts, William, 116
Roosevelt, President Franklin D., 47
Rodd, F. R., 158
Ross, Sir James, 34

Rowe, Margaret (daughter), 63, 68, 69, 70, 83, 111, 120, 174
Rowe, Samuel, 25, 111
Royal Georgie, 155
Royal Institution of Cornwall, 158, 159
Russell, Rev Jack, 79

Sabine, General Sir Edward, 34
St Barnabas church, Pimlico, 32
Scott, Sir Walter, 134
Sessay, 51
Sharp, Cecil, 87, 129, 136-8, 168
Sharp, Rev John, 43, 44, 56, 58
Sheppard, Rev H. Fleetwood, 128, 134, 141
Silver Poplar', 'The, 15
Silver Store, The, 59
Song-men (alphabetical list), 130-32
Songs of the West, 128, 135, 136, 138, 139
Southey, Robert, 25
Sperling, H, 80, 120, 166
Sperling, Mrs, 80, 121
Staverton, 14, 67, 68
Story of the Nations, The, 153
Swinburne, Algernon Charles, 64
Sullivan, Sir Arthur, 47, 142
Sydenham House, 108

Tavistock, 21, 108
Teck, Duke of, 154
Tennyson, Alfred, Lord, 150
Three Drunken Maidens, The (folk-song), 135
Through Flood and Flame, 56, 57, 64
Through the Night of Doubt and Sorrow (hymn), 48, 174
Tinley, Cicely (daughter), 64, 88, 165
Tinley, Col F. Newport, 88
Tinley, Gervaise, DFC, 88
Topcliffe, 51
Tractarian Movement, 29, 31, 32, 52, 101
Tragedy of the Caesars, The, 152

Vicar of Morwenstowe, The, 149

Index

Warwick Grammar School, 19
Westington, Arthur, 12
Widdicombe Fair (folk-song), 125
Widdicombe, Irene (niece), 12, 95, 162
Wilberforce, Samuel (Bishop), 37, 60

Whitwell, Rev W. J., 156
Wuthering Heights, 64

'Year of Revolutions', 222
Yorkshire Characters and Strange Events, 151